Vision in the Dark

HOW LIVING IN THE DARK
TAUGHT ME TO SEE THE LIGHT

Dr. Andre Watson

Dr. Andre Watson
313 South 16th Street
Philadelphia, PA 19102
www.visioninthedark.com

Ordering Information:
Quantity sales. Special discounts are available on quantity purchases by
corporations, associations, and others. For details, contact the "Special
Sales Department" at the address above.

Vision in the Dark/Dr. Andre Watson
ISBN 978-0692760253

Contents

DEDICATION

To my mother, Gladys Watson, who is the embodiment of love, sacrifice, and determination. This book is dedicated to you. You loved Le'Nell and me, sacrificed everything you had for us, and you were determined to raise us on your own in a world that did not give us a chance. You wove into the fabric of my being the love for hard work, humility, stubborn optimism, and an undying spirit to fight life's challenges head-on. Mom, I love you. Your love gave me what I needed to be able to see, even though I am a blind man.

To my dear wife, Katina: this book is dedicated to you. Thank you for believing in me. You believe in me as a colleague, friend, husband, and father. I could be nothing without your love, support, and encouragement. Thank you for daring to dream with me. We are conquering the world together. For your belief in me has allowed me to see the world's greatest beauties. I see your gorgeousness and the adorableness of our daughter because of your awe-some insights and your love for me.

To my sister Le'Nell, this book is dedicated to you. Just like Mom, you have been through every-thing with me from the beginning, even before the time you remember. Your spirit always radiated precious love as a young baby and now as a woman. You taught me about tenderness and relationship, and prepared me to be a father and husband. You have treated me as the person I am. You have al-ways seen me as just Andre, and because of you, I can see myself.

To my family, this book is dedicated to you. You all prayed for me, loved me, and most importantly kept me well fed when you did not know what more to do. That's fine, because my happiness and com-fort was always a priority. To my grandparents, aunts, uncles and cousins, you all have meant so much to me. Because of your love for me, I can see.

To every teacher and supervisor I have ever had, this book is dedicated to you. If you decided to be my teacher, then you believed in me too. Many re-fused to teach me, but you believed I could succeed. Your vision for me also helped me to see. You helped make me the psychologist I am today.

To every coach, teammate, and opponent I have ever had, this book is dedicated to you. You saw more than just a blind kid or visually impaired man, but you saw a champion. You saw a formidable athlete. You showed me how powerful and strong I was, both inside and outside of the gym. Because of you, I can see. With you I became determined to never quit and to never say die, no matter the challenge.

To every friend who took a chance to speak to me, this book is for you. You saw more than just a disability when you met me, but you saw that I had life inside of me. You came up to me on the first day of school, or in the cafeteria, or on the way home to the bus stop. Instead of dismissing me, you validated my existence and saw fun, laughter, and connection. Because of you, I see.

Last but not least, I want to thank Omar and Jéneen Barlow, who helped to concretely pull my story out of me. Both of you have been a coach in telling my story. You both are visionaries. You two knew that I had a story to tell before I even told you my story. Thank you for your leadership, passion for life, and for living on purpose. Because of you, I see myself more clearly, and through this book, my readers, patients, and audiences can see me too.

"But He said to me, 'My grace is sufficient for you, for power is perfected in weakness.' Therefore, I will most gladly boast all the more about my weaknesses, so that Christ's power may reside in me."

—II Corinthians 12:9

Introduction

Thirty years ago, Andre Watson's life changed drastically. Growing up, he was always told to "shoot for the stars," to be whatever he wanted to be. Originally, society told him implicitly and explicitly that he could be a distinguished doctor, an amazing athlete, a profound professor, a fantastic father, a limitless leader, a sensational success; just "believe it and then you will see it! Everyone has a chance to be whatever they want to be." But what happens when you don't "see your way," literally and figuratively? At the age of nine, Andre was diagnosed as being legally blind. After over a dozen surgeries to save his eyesight, his family had to face the inevitable: their dear Babyboy was going to lose his sight.

Which way do you go when your world is turned upside down? What do you do when your life takes a seemingly downward turn? What do you do with your life when "bad things happen?" So many people look at the negative odds, listen to the pessimistic "experts," and fail to fulfill their purpose. The failure comes from over relying on physical sight and doubting the power of internal vision. Over relying on Physical Sight leads to stagnation, only focuses on immediate and present circumstances, and narrowly lends attention to the surface. Conversely, relying on a vision helps us to be dynamic, see into the future, and see hidden potential.

Andre could have internalized the doubts and short sightedness of this "sighted" world that relentlessly worships their eyes for false senses of protection, security, and certainty. Fortunately, even though Andre lost his sight, he did not lose his vision of himself, his purpose, and of life. Once he realized that true sight came from within, his vision for his life and for the life of others became clearer than ever. Paradoxically, it was after he was led into the dark, he could see "the light." With the lessons that his life has given him, he is now sharing those lessons with his audiences, his patients, his colleagues, his readers, and anyone in this world who is brave enough to close their eyes, so that they might see.

Vision in the dark is a book about how when the odds are against you and when no one can see how you can "do it," it's up to you to have an internal vision, an eternal light, and a never dying spirit that surpasses the limitations of physical sight. Would you believe it if someone told you that their blind doctor could "see" where they were coming from? Would you believe it if a blind athlete had perfect positioning and pinpoint accuracy? Would you believe it to hear about a blind husband who finds his wife stunning without ever seeing her face? And if you found all of these features amazing or admirable, wouldn't you want to possess the essence of that character? The hard question is, "Would you be willing to give your physical sight up to really see?" The truth is that all of us, whether we are physically sighted or not, have to learn how to look beyond the physical, and look to the most vulnerable parts of the self to find vision and purpose.

Dr. Watson is a clinical psychologist, athlete, scholar, husband, and father who is physically blind, but has clear sight in the psychological, emotional, and spiritual realms of life. Read this story to see how Dr. Watson developed his own identity based on what he saw in himself on the inside rather than what others see on the outside. Dr. Watson's triumphs over the impossible are not just uniquely his, but for everyone who never gives up and who uses more than just their physical eyes to see their purpose, destiny, and path in life. Vision in the dark is a true story that teaches all of us to forget what you can physically see and to focus on your vision to be more than you ever would imagine, especially during life's supposed misfortunes.

CHAPTER 1

Seeing in the Dark

I felt myself getting choked up, and my breathing became staggered. My shoulders started to shake, and my neck stiffened as his voice penetrated my cool, composed exterior. Tears started running down my face. "Wow, he sounds just like he did on the day I graduated from this high school ten years ago," I thought to myself. He always spoke with a deliberate, monotonous cadence, as if to make sure that every word was grammatically and phonetically perfect—and, most importantly, obeyed. Each syllable that came out of his mouth was important—at least, that's what it seemed like.

I'd halfheartedly listened to what he had to say during assemblies as a carefree teenager, but his words on this day, a later graduation ceremony at my alma mater, will echo in my heart forever. I was going to give a keynote address, and get the chance to speak to these young people. For some reason, what I had to say was "important," and my life story was worth telling. I tried to remember what I was going to say while listening attentively to the principal. My thoughts and emotions kept pulling my attention away. I was nervous, but filled with passion to tell my story so that someone else could be encouraged, as well.

"Today is a special day," he said to his students. "I want you all to listen closely, listen carefully, and listen well. Pay attention," Dr. Pavel commanded. The students were quiet. They were paying attention. My high school principal then started talking about me. He told today's students all about my accomplishments while attending Central High School in Philadelphia a decade earlier, and how I had been 2004's Athletic Hall of Fame inductee that year. He told them his thoughts and feelings about all I had achieved. He had often appeared to me as a strict, no nonsense, perfectionistic man, but today, he was more open—softer and more expressive. Memorably, he said to my mother, who was in the audience, "Thank you. Thank you for sharing your son with us." That was when the tears started running down my face. Memories of my life were coming back to me as a slideshow of feelings.

I felt an overwhelming rush of flooding emotion, and was touched with thankfulness and gratitude that my terrified mother had shared me with the world—and the world had let me in. Most mothers would not have allowed their "baby" to venture out into the world. Many would have chosen to hide me, and protect me from any more hurt.

Going to Central High School changed my life. It gave me the opportunity to receive the best education any "inner-city youth" could get. It gave me the chance to compete academically with the smartest, brightest kids in the country. Even though I was different from most of the brothers growing up in Philadelphia, I was even more different from the brothers who were going to Central. Kids who attended there were smart, and knew how to excel academically. Many of them were from the city, and knew how to handle themselves interpersonally, as well. It was not uncommon for my peer group to ask "What's up?" and "What's the square route of i?" in the same conversation. People who went to Central had a blend of book smarts and street smarts. Some of us had more of one than the other, but the point is, we were cool, we were smart, and we were balanced.

I was a black boy with some smarts and some social skills, but I had additional challenges. Not only did I have to compete academically and find ways to make friends socially, I also had to learn how to navigate a world that designed for sighted people. Going to Central meant I'd have to find a way to get along when I was different from everyone else around me. I lived in the dark. I was blind.

All my life, I've approached new challenges with a certain determination and stubbornness cloaked in patience, humor, and coolness—while deep down inside, I was fighting self-doubt in addition to the doubts of others. Going to Central helped me learn the value of believing in myself and appreciating those who believed in me. Central gave me a chance: to fulfill my purpose in life, and to be everything I had wanted to be before losing my eyesight at the age of nine. Even though I had been given a chance, it was my responsibility to walk through the door of opportunity that opened in front of me.

Central gave me something invaluable and intangible. In spite of the odds working against me, Central believed in me. When someone believes in you, you can achieve anything. My mother has always believed in me; she believed in me even before I was born. She told me that she expected and hoped that I'd be someone special one day: a fireman, lawyer, police officer, judge, or even a professional football player. Whatever it was, my mother knew I was going to be good at anything—just as any believing mother should.

When I was born, my mother was positive about my future success. She had been the first in her family to go to college and finish. My mother was a health and physical education teacher for 40 years in the Philadelphia School District—and when you say the "Philadelphia School District," that's code for "she was a super teacher." The teachers in the Philadelphia School District were not only teachers, but also disciplinarians, counselors, lay therapists, nurses, and parent substitutes. My mother has a loud and commanding presence, and a voice to back it up. When you're a gym teacher, you're also a cheerleader, referee, coach, mentor, sergeant, and judge. She knew that education was a priority in my life, and that with education, nothing could stop me. Before I lost my eyesight, the world gave me a half a chance, because, after all, I was still a black boy. After I lost my eyesight, I changed from a "half-chance" to a "whole charity."

At the age of seven and a half, the trajectory of my life changed. I had been encouraged by so many to shoot for the stars. My mother had taught me well. If anyone asked what I wanted to be, I said something impressive, like a doctor or a lawyer; but after I started to lose something seemingly irreplaceable—my eyesight—we did not know what to expect.

The administrators at Central High School knew the gamble they were taking when they accepted me. It was a sink-or-swim culture, and many of us did not survive. My ninth-grade class started with 700 or 800 students, but less than 500 made it. Some of the students barely survived, and others glided through. A few of my friends are now very successful teachers, lawyers, journalists, doctors, and businesspeople, but many of those smart and successful people struggled through Central High School. They went to summer school, spent countless hours studying, and shed blood, sweat, and tears, only to barely finish at our school.

My path as a blind kid was no easier. For every hour my classmates studied, I studied at least two. My trip home was twice as long, because my mother insisted that I catch the Route C and 21 buses instead of the subway and elevated trains, which would have cut my commute in half. This meant I had to get up earlier than my peers, and arrive home later than they did, as well. On top of that, I wanted to have fun. I joined the wrestling team, attended every dance and prom I could, and chatted on the phone with friends for countless hours.

My mother, Gladys Watson, was afraid to allow her blind son to explore the world without her: "He was vulnerable, he was untested, and he was literally in the dark." For her to share me with the world, she had to face the reality that I was in physical darkness, and that panicked her. Her son could not see cars coming. He would not be able to evade shifty, unsavory hoodlums lurking in the streets. Her baby was unable to visually watch for construction, poles blocking his path, or manholes ready to swallow him up. Her son would be unable to find his way, and getting lost would always be a possibility. To her, being alone and in the dark meant that my safety was compromised, and that I was always in some potential danger.

My mother was an excellent teacher. Her most familiar arenas were those relating to sports, volleyball, basketball, and softball. A common problem for her to solve might have involved reaching some angry, neglected kid. An ordinary issue to face might have included an irate parent yelling at her and intimidating her. The impossible problem, though, was to allow her only son to venture into the dark. She welcomed a shooting guard taking a risk to steal the ball from an opponent, but a risk for her son to cross the street by himself was horrifying. She encouraged her athletes to fight aggressively and win, but she worried that her son could not fight. My mother pulled the best out of her athletes, and expected them to give it their all in the game. She shouted, yelled, and believed in them. Most importantly, she never let a deserving kid sit on the bench.

Even though she was absolutely paralyzed with fear about her son growing up in the world, it went against every fiber in her being to allow him to sit on the bench. Metaphorically, I had the potential to dribble on the court, legs to stand on, and the passion to win the game—I just couldn't see. In life, Mom put me in the game not only to play, but to win. She shared me with the rest of the world, and I am forever thankful to her for being my life coach.

Not only did she share me with Central, she also put me in the game of life—and made me a starter. My mother was the first person to give me a chance to succeed. She believed in me.

My old principal called me up to the podium. I was already losing my composure. How could I speak while overcome with raw emotion? I stood up from where I had been sitting just behind the podium, and he guided me to the stand. I placed my hands on either side of its wooden surface, but I could not speak. My mouth opened, but no air came out. I was choked by my emotions. I heard my principal's voice behind me: "Breathe." He gave me a command, and I pulled myself out of that ocean of deep sensation and turned it into pure passion. I began to speak.

"Even though I will never know many of you, you are all family to me." My voice fought to come out of my tightened chest. "You have all joined a legacy of excellence. You all have been chosen to do something special in life. You all have a purpose. It wasn't too long ago that I was here. Man, this place smells the same." The students laughed. "And I know what else hasn't changed: your greatness! No matter who you are, where you're from, or what color you are—black, white, Asian, Native American, Jewish, Christian, Muslim, whatever—you are special. Teachers, thank you for teaching these students. Please nurture them and take care of them, and give them the same as you gave me—a chance—because they are all the best of the best." This was the chance I had been given that made me who I am today. Many teachers had known that this black blind boy had potential, and they knew I needed that chance. I knew that with courage, I could outwork anyone who challenged me.

My mother is a superhero. A single mother even when she was married, she did it all. By example, she showed my sister and me how to work long hours; in doing so, she was able to buy her children their favorite toys for Christmas that they had been waiting for all year long. My mother did not have any help from my biological father, as they had split up when I was under the age of four. The stress of being discriminated against as a black man ate him alive, and as a result, he lashed out at others, including my mother. My stepfather seemed to be wrestling with his own demons—drugs, sex, and rock 'n' roll as a 70s hippy—and that kept him from really helping my mother when she needed him. Instead, she pushed herself, and she pushed her children.

She always taught me to be independent, I think because she had been disappointed so many times in her life. She had also seen how life had beaten down the two men from whom she had wanted more. Life's trials, pressures, and injustices had prevented them from reaching their potential as fathers and partners. Her own mother and father had also sacrificed everything for my mother and her four siblings. She knew the power of love, and how passion could push anyone into supernatural strength.

I continued on: "This school made me who I am because someone gave me a chance. Someone gave me a chance to excel, to make a mistake, to be myself—but that wasn't the end of it. I took every opportunity that was in front of me. I never said 'I can't' or 'I won't.' There were plenty of other people doing that for me. Instead, I decided to prove the world wrong, and show them the power of the human spirit. And all of you have that power, that ability."

I will always be grateful for the day I was the keynote speaker at Central High's Hall of Fame Ceremony. My life story was becoming crystal clear. Even though I am physically blind, my vision was not blurry, cloudy, or hazy; I could see. I could see the important lessons in life, all because so many people decided to give me a chance.

Unfortunately, not everyone gets a chance, and there have been many people who have not given me one. They have been overwhelmed with misunderstandings of my world, believing that living "in the dark" means that one cannot see at all. I've noticed that some strangers are uncomfortable around me. They are unsure of what to say, or how to say it.

Talk becomes stiff, voices get unusually soft or loud, and body language is sometimes a little bit closer or farther away. Gauging how to interact with me seems to be a chore for some people.

Do I say the word "see" around a blind man? Do I let him walk into a closed door? What if he can't understand what I'm talking about when I talk about movies? Did he see that football game? The Eagles looked good—I mean sounded good—I mean performed...I'm not sure what I mean.

Comments like these represent just a small fraction of the questions I have heard from patients and people brave enough to tell me about their reactions to interacting with me for the first time, before they got to know me well. In short, many of them were afraid.

My hypothesis is that fear tends to be at the core of many reactions to blindness. Physical blindness denotes the inability to see with the eyes, but it can signify so much more. Blindness means an inability to see something, and thus an inability to understand. Blindness connotes doing something without preparation. It suggests ignorance and illogical thinking—the opposite of scientific. It suggests being unaware, easily taken advantage of, or not having a purpose. It signifies a lack of knowledge. For me, I believe that the most salient stereotype of blindness is that blindness represents an absence of light.

Light illuminates, gives clarity, exposes the dark, and brings understanding. Light is good...the opposite of bad. Light comes out during the day, and signifies a new beginning. Light shows you the path to heaven, to nirvana—the righteous path. On the other hand, darkness is a polarized metaphor for all things not light-like. With regard to awareness, darkness hides the truth, deceives vision, and conceals evidence. Darkness hides the unknown. Darkness does not allow us to see. It blinds us. Darkness shows you nothing.

As for those who never gave me a chance, I believe they are the people who really could not see. I believe that sight is possessed by someone who knows what's around them. Possession of sight means that one has clarity in their life, and insight into the lives of others. I believe that having sight means possessing the knowledge, wisdom, and courage to live with a purpose. Having sight means you can see through the superficial and perceive the internal. It means that one can make their dreams seen on the level of the external, and therefore possess a vision of the eternal. Having sight means that what really matters is in clear view, and what isn't important is looked past. Having sight means you can really see!

So many of my patients have come to me asking for help with improving and perfecting their sight, but they don't mean their physical sight. They ask for insight and understanding about why they do the things they do. They ask for insight into gaining greater understanding of their children. They ask for revelations about their marriages. They ask that their eyes be opened to their life's purpose. Over the years, at so many times and on so many occasions, my patients have expressed thankfulness that I have not physical sight, but internal sight. My ability to see the internal workings of a situation, in spite of external factors, makes them trust me, believe in me, and close their eyes in order to be more like me.

I remember a session with one of my patients: "I have my eyes closed right now. You cannot see, so I am going to try to just listen. And that's why I picked you—because I figured that you wouldn't look at me and judge me. I've been overweight all my life, but you wouldn't be looking at me. Instead, you'd be paying attention to my heart, my mind, my soul. And I wasn't wrong," he laughed. "I had so much shame before I came to you. I didn't like anyone to look at me. I have done things that I am ashamed of, and I can't even bear to look at myself in the mirror—but after working with you, I can see myself for who I really am, and it feels good."

This patient highlighted the way in which many of us put physical sight on a pedestal. We judge others based upon what we can see physically. We don't take time to see the internal—or the eternal—but instead take the easy way out. We depend upon that which is right in front of us.

Being in the dark has given me a clearer vision of life. I have learned that what you see is not always what you get. Many people have given me a chance, but others judged a book by its cover. They thought their two physical eyes were more powerful than my third one. My cover appeared plain, cheap, and unofficial. My closed eyes seemed dim, and my blindness gave the impression of vulnerability; but they were using their physical sight. The people who have doubted me the most have often been the ones with the least amount of insight. The ones who believe that I can see what's important are the most insightful people.

When I was born, I had perfect vision—at least physically. I lived the life of a typical child. I liked to watch television. My favorite 80s television shows were *Knight Rider, Voltron,* and *V.* I loved to act like a superhero, and I liked drawing them even more: Superman, Spiderman, and Batman were some of my favorites. "Wow, look how strong Spiderman is in this picture!" I would say to my mother when I was eight years old. "Mom, look at this picture. It's Superman flying!" I'd exclaim, or "Wow, Batman is a cool guy!" These superheroes were my childhood idols. I wanted to be amazing like them, and act courageously; and, even when it was most difficult, to do the right thing.

In many ways, after I lost my sight, people didn't seem to give me a chance to be a hero. I was given a pass when it came to doing something extraordinary. I was told I could be less than ordinary. When it was time to be courageous, people were encouraging me not to face fear; and when I wanted to do the right thing, I was told, in a number of ways, that I did not have to do anything. This adversity could have changed my identity, but it did not. As a child growing up, I was taught to believe in myself and everything I could achieve. My mother did not raise me to be a superhero, but she did raise me to have all of the characteristics that any hero has. I was told I could do anything!

My mother pushed me to be a "good boy," love God, strive for excellence in school, and shoot for the stars in my career because she knew the realities of being a black man. Her father, my grandfather, had been a hardworking welder at the Philadelphia Navy Base. My mother said he worked hard for his family and to put food on the table. She said he spent long days getting up at 5 a.m. and going to bed at 11 p.m., only to do it all over again the next day. In his diligence and devotion, he showed her how to raise me. She knew that I would have to work harder than my peers if I hoped to be success-ful. If people thought she had pushed me before my eyesight went, I can tell you that she was shoving me afterwards.

When I was about seven years old, I loved to play hard on the playground. I didn't mind getting dirty, ripping holes in my clothes, or scraping the palms of my hands on the ground. In the second and third grades, I went to Commodore John Barry Elementary School in West Philadelphia. I loved it. It was my first experience of male camaraderie. The best days were the fall mornings when we had "extra recess." Recess was never long enough. Just as soon as you got started, it was time to go inside; but once in a while, Mr. Davis, the stern, bald, brown-skinned, intimidating vice principal, became benevolent. He would blow the whistle and demand that we all get into line. The boys and girls lined up separately. When the boys knew they were going to get extra recess, they stood in the straightest line you've ever seen. We would space ourselves out by putting our hands on the boy's shoulders in front of us to make sure the spacing was perfect. Then we stood with our feet together and arms straight down at our sides. We were like rows of toy soldiers. Wow, that felt tough. We tried not to move a muscle. We had to hold that pose until Mr. Davis had worked his way down the rows of lines of children and inspected our posture and formation. When the general approved of his little toy soldiers, he gave the okay for us to commence playing.

Sometimes, we played wall ball with somebody's old tennis ball. At other times, we played a football-like game with my brown-and-white lunch pail. My mother would have killed me if she knew I was letting my friends run up and down with that lunchbox as if she had the money to buy a new one. Some of my friends were really fast, and we all imagined we were like the pros: bobbing, weaving, and juking. Some of those guys were great at it—so fast, so quick, they could juke their way past 11 boys, all the way to the other end of the playground. We all stretched out to catch that one fast kid, but his head fakes to the left made us all shift that way to open up his lane to the right. He could stop on a dime. That fastest kid was Jared. Wow, did we all want to be like him. One of my best friends was named Dana. He was a thick, round kid. He and I liked to race, and man, for a chunky kid, he could run pretty fast.

At other times, we pretended to box and hit each other. One guy who thought he was tough would pretend to punch kids in the eye. Well, one day, he hit me. It didn't hurt—it just made my eye feel like someone had poked it. That was when my eye problems began. I rubbed and rubbed it after being poked. I didn't make a big deal about it. I went to the school nurse to show her, but she was in a rush. "Oh, son, just keep blinking it," she said, as she rushed out of her office on the way to some other meeting.

A few days passed, and my eye was red from all the rubbing. I had contracted pinkeye. My mother took me to the doctor, and we were told that it would go away. Then, something weird happened. I woke up and couldn't see anything out of my right eye. I was scared and confused, and didn't know what was wrong. My mother was terrified. She does not do well with fear. Usually, she compensates by feeling anger.

"I hope you aren't lying to me," she told me sternly on the way to the hospital. Deep down inside, though, she hoped I was lying to her. She hoped that her son was playing a joke, or wanted attention, or that she was just dreaming. The doctor told us that I would need surgery because I had a major infection in my eye.

My surgeries were full of so much pain, and they didn't just cause pain in my eye—my head hurt, my body ached, and my throat was sore. I was completely wiped out. Surgery took so much energy out of me.

We thought the first surgery was actually a success. Afterward, I was able to see, but something unusual started to happen. I continued to have eye problems, which led to multiple retina detachments in my right eye; and then, strangely, they spread to my left eye. My clear vision—sun, grass, wooden swings on a playground, monkey bars and blue cloudless skies—slowly turned into an experience that was more like looking through a narrow peep-hole or monocular. The difference was that I was not able to see better—in fact, my vision worsened. The darkness of blindness slowly closed in over my visual view of the world. Between the ages of seven and 11, I had had 13 operations. I went through 13 procedures with sleeping gas, multiple needles, blood draws, and eye patches. For some unexplain-able reason, I lost my hearing after one operation. I found myself in cloudy darkness and muffled tun-nels, trying to hear and trying to see. It's no wonder that at one juncture, I was rushed by ambulance af-ter surgery to Children's Hospital of Philadelphia for skyrocketing high blood pressure. I was proba-bly stressed out. I was losing my sight.

In December of 1985, just before Christmas, I ex-perienced a terrible retinal detachment. Just before that setback, I still had some useable vision, and was getting around with a thick pair of strong pre-scription sunglasses. My school had changed, and I was going to Overbrook Educational Center. They wisely started teaching me Braille, because my eye-sight was so unstable.

That day, I had gone to school as usual and no-ticed the familiar floaters that signified a detachment. My world was blurry, hazy, fuzzy, and confusing. I strained with all I had in my left eye. I told my teachers, Mrs. Peters and Ms. Smith, that I couldn't see. They called my mother. I went to the hospital with her again, and we prepared for another time on the operating table. We didn't know if it would be a success. My family was praying that God would have mercy on their nine-year-old Andre.

After a retinal reattachment, the eye has to be shut for quite some time in order to heal. I had to wear a patch over my eye, and it was hard to focus. When I tried, my eye would roll to the back of my head and gush with tears. It was swollen and hard to open. The only way I could open it was with my fingers, very gently and carefully. It hurt so much to do that, but I needed to for the medications I had been given to help the healing process.

Boy, I was in pain all over. After that surgery, I had to be in the hospital for nearly a week to recover. While there, my mother said to me, "Andre, Mommy needs to tell you something," and then she paused. "The doctor thinks that...you might not be able to see again." I was sitting on the doctor's table, and my legs were dangling. I felt a rush of tears come to both of my eyes at that point. I was devastated. The first thing I thought of was that I would never get to play with my friends on the playground again. I'd never be able to draw a superhero again. I'd never be able to become a professional athlete. I cried hard. My mother hugged me, and pulled me close to her. She started to cry, but she kept her composure. She was strong, but I know she wanted to fall on the floor. She wanted to die. To think of her son losing his sight was one of the most terrifying things for her. My mother has since told me that the thought of me being "in the dark" still scares her terribly. She imagines it as the most excruciating thing someone could ever go through. How was I going to find my way in the world? How was I going to "do for myself?" How was I going to live? All of these questions were hers already, as the mother of a black boy—but now they were multiplied for her black, blind boy. She had no clue how I was going to survive.

As I mentioned earlier, if my mother feels fear, it comes out as anger. Well, needless to say, she was an angry mother. Over the years, it came out as yelling, lashing out, or screaming; but many times, it also came out as a fortified strength that she poured into me. "You now have three strikes against you," my mother preached. "You are black, you are blind, and you are a black man." She started a boot camp-like persona with me. When many parents would have just thrown in the towel and held their poor little baby, she didn't. When other parents would have given the child up to someone else to raise, my mother refused. When other parents would have thrown up their hands in defeat, my mother refused to lose her son. When the world was not sure what to do with me, my mother told me what to do with myself: I should never, ever give up. I should die before giving up, because giving up was as bad as dying. Many such people live in this world, and they are the walking dead. My mother taught me to strive and press toward the mark.

She became a drill sergeant around the house. The parents of some of my friends cleaned their rooms for them. Not this black mama. She insisted that I clean it—and so did I. I had been expected to do chores before losing my sight, and I took pride in doing a good job. I beamed when my grandmother bragged about me doing the dishes for her. I loved to help carry groceries into a neighbor's home. I stuck my chest out when giving up my seat on the bus to an older person. I had felt pride as a sighted kid, and I wanted that to continue. Luckily—and sometimes, not so luckily—my mother held me to that standard.

She expected the same out of me as she would have if I could see. I was expected to study, do well in school, and do my chores—and, most of all, remain respectful to her and our home. Being blind was not an excuse. She made sure I was aware of myself and how I appeared to others. "Pick your head up! Smile! Make sure your clothes are neat!" My mother loved me beyond measure. She would have died before giving up on me.

As a psychologist, I feel my mother's passion for life flowing through my veins as I work with my patients. I never give up on anyone. No matter how long it takes someone to gain insight, get their feet back under them, or rebound from life's hardships, my mother's voice still echoes in my mind. "Do not give up. God does not make mistakes." Some of my patients are religious, and others are not; but for each and every one of them, I believe they are living for a reason. My purpose in life is to help them obtain clearer vision in their own lives. It is an honor for me to be given an opportunity of this kind.

One of my favorite patients, who was intellectually disabled and also visually impaired, told me something so insightful. "You know, Dr. Watson, when we started working together, I made many excuses for myself. I often told people that I could not do things because I was blind—but you are blind, and you do so much stuff. I realized that I don't have an "eye" problem; it's an IQ problem." This patient and I spent a lot of time together talking about the direction of her life, and she turned out to be one of the smartest people I was working with. She realized that it was not physical vision that was her barrier, but negative self-talk. She had grown up as a kid in special education. She had been teased, and called "slow" and "good-for-nothing." She was spoken to in a patronizing way. She was supposed to be "not the brightest crayon in the box," but she had made the most insightful comment to me, and verbalized what many people don't understand. A person's ability to physically see is not important if they can mentally see. And when you can see what is most important, nothing can stop you. My patients see that in me, even when I haven't told them a thing about myself. When they see a black, blind man sitting in front of them, they know that my life has not been easy. I have had to devise other ways of living. I did not give up after losing my sight, but instead, went deeper into my darkness.

This helped me to face fears, build courage, and look for true sight. I believe my patients do the same, even if they are not physically blind. I help them go into the scary part of life: inside of themselves. Inside us are our fears, our love, our hate, our disgusting feelings, our traumas, our memories, our dreams, and our hopes. That is frightening to face. In the darkness, my patients close their physical eyes forget what they see, and focus on what they believe. I refuse the line of thought that "seeing something is believing," and change it to "believing something is seeing something." If people don't believe in themselves, they don't see what they are capable of doing. If people don't have someone who believes in them, they don't have anyone shining light into their lives. Some people live in spiritual darkness who can physically see, because they have lost sight of who they are and their life's purpose.

One of the most difficult parts of experiencing a significant loss in life is understanding why. Life is filled with so many tragedies, unforeseen catastrophes, and heartbreaks. So many people ask God, the universe, or other people, "Why did this happen to me?" Life's body blows can rock someone's whole self-concept and personal sense of meaning. Many of the people I have seen over the years have lost loved ones, relationships, abilities, careers, and status. The list goes on and on. What they see in me is the ability to lose one momentous thing (my sight), and to use that loss to gain something bigger in life. I have a career, I have a family, I have a passion for life, and I have an undying spirit.

When life's circumstances fall into the status quo—ordinary and comfortable—we don't have a reason to change. When "life happens," we have to change. My blindness made me different, with flexibilities I am now using in my entire life. When life is unclear and blurry, I don't panic. I know that perseverance through cloudy paths and murky waters will make me more patient and courageous. It's always so easy to move forward when we know what the outcome will be—but what do we do when WE ARE IN THE DARK? What do we do when we are afraid? Oftentimes, we give up and quit. My blindness has helped me to sharpen my skills of patience and courage.

I am patient when I don't always know what is literally ahead of me. I am courageous when I physically take steps forward. I have exercised patience and courage as I have ventured on many life journeys. I am a licensed psychologist. I have traveled around the world: to Asia, South America, Europe, and all over the United States. I am an accomplished, international athlete. I have challenged myself to learn martial arts and compete against sighted opponents over the past 25 years, and I stepped out on a limb to find my wife.

When you are courageous enough to walk forward in the dark in spite of fear, you are getting emotionally and spiritually stronger. That strength can help you to overcome future obstacles, conquer fears, and achieve your dreams. Walking in the dark is not just literal, for me—it is also figurative. Walking in the dark requires courage, faith, patience, and humility. Walking in the dark is not easy. In life, we have to know how to wait, how to take chances, how to believe in ourselves, and how to be open to learning.

And this is what I do. I teach my patients how to walk in the dark. I teach them how to see with another set of eyes. Their physical sight distracts with doubt. I help them to develop their third eye, their internal sight, their inner person.

CHAPTER 2

Praying in the Dark

I had just tapped my way into Troy's Chop Shop at 60th and Market for my biweekly haircut, and walking up to the door, I could sense it. I smelled the mixture of scents you get when you go into an African-American barbershop. It smells like hair mixed with a lot of Sea Breeze, the fragrances of hairsprays and shampoos, and a hint of electric razor. I could hear enthusiastic voices speaking in the rhythmic cadence of brotherhood.

I enjoyed going to Troy's Chop Shop, because it was my first taste of male bonding. It was "all that." I often laughed at the gut-busting, hilarious stories told. I cackled whenever playful bravado was on display, and I was always tentatively listening when wisdom and encouragement were passed out for free to anyone who could hear them over the music coming from the stereo. Before Troy's Chop Shop, I was getting my hair cut at a hair salon down the street from my grandmother's house, by Karen at

Mrs. Melton's Beauty Salon. My mother usually got her hair done, then I got my hair done. Or rather...I got my hair cut. Guys don't get their hair done—just cut. When my cousin Troy got wind that I was getting my hair done, sitting under the dryer, using conditioners, and getting a regular dose of Oprah Winfrey with the old ladies, he recommended that I come down to the shop with "the boys."

Most times, when I stepped into the Chop Shop, I got a round of "Yo, what's up?" from everyone. In the barbershop, you're somebody—once they know your name and decide you're friendly and not fake. When I stepped in, I was usually well greeted by the crowd as I sat down. Well, one day in my early 20s, something different happened.

I walked in with my cane tapping, my eyes partially closed, as they usually are, and a smile on my face. I had started to get rounds of "Yo, what's up?" when a small boy yelled out, "Daddy, it's a monster!" I heard his voice projecting right at me. "It's the monster, Daddy! It's the monster!" I'm guessing the boy's father was slightly embarrassed as he tried to hush his son. "No, boy, he's not a monster. That's not a monster." I guess I felt a little better— now I wasn't a monster, just a "that." Even though his dad tried to console him, he was convinced that he probably saw death. The boy cried and screamed. I just sat down and hoped that my haircut would begin quickly. Maybe he was talking about someone else. Maybe he was talking about me. Was I the monster? By my 20s, I was learning that people saw me so much differently than I saw myself. I saw myself as a ball of potential rolling along through life and collecting speed, but others saw me as an oddity—a that, a thing, something without potential. I felt embarrassed, and prayed that he was not talking about me. I just pretended not to be phased, and sat and waited for my hair to be cut.

The boy sounded like he was about three or four years old. Eventually, he calmed down. His father started talking to another gentleman in the Chop Shop. "Yeah, it's probably because I put that mud mask on my face at night and did this: GUR! GUR!" I imagined him making an ugly face to scare his son. By the sound of his voice, I pictured his eyes squinting, his teeth biting, and lips poked out on a mashed-up face. Who knows— someone could have been getting a facial at the Chop Shop...or that little boy could have been looking at me. At the time, I just knew it was me.

My experience with people had always been colored by fear, gloom, and doom, and I figured this was it all over again. It was possible that somehow, the boy had confused my smiling face, my cane, and my squinting eyes as the horrifying features of a monster.

As I think back at that moment, I laugh. Sometimes, I bring it up around some of my blind friends, and many of them crack up laughing. They usually say something like, "That boy was right. You really are a monster! Look what you did to that poor child!" I just insist halfheartedly that the boy had been screaming in horror about someone else.

Now, as an adult and psychologist, I rub my metaphorical, investigative chin and analyze it. Am I a monster? I think about the various reactions I get when I go into public places, and when I meet new people. I think about when I used to date. Fear always seemed to loom close by. People didn't yell out, "Look at the monster," but they treated me as if I were one. They distanced themselves from me, paralyzed by fear; seemed afraid of getting too close to me, as if I would bite; patronized me out of pity; or treated me as if I would snap if they broke the rules of etiquette. Scenes of Young Frankenstein, The Elephant Man, and Mask often pop into my mind when I walk down the city streets of Philadelphia. As I approach chattering people, their chatter comes to an abrupt halt once I get too close—and once I clear the scene, the chatter begins again. It's like walking past grasshoppers on a warm summer evening. They chirp, chirp, chirp, but just as you approach them, they stop, hoping that you won't find them. When you pass, the chirping starts up again. To me, people's talking is also a bit like a cassette tape playing. As I loom closer, the talking hits pause; and when I pass, the play button resumes.

What is going on? Do my blind eyes beg for the captive stares of others? Does my blindness attract unsolicited attention? Am I the "other?" Am I a foreign entity? Or am I like the freak at a sideshow? Does my difference draw wonder and mystery out of people? Does my cane or method of travel evoke fears surrounding safety? Does my blindness concern others?

It's not uncommon for my wife and I to go out for dinner, and we notice that waiters, waitresses, and servers avoid interacting with me. Here's what happens. We go to a restaurant and are seated. We look at the menu. Sometimes, this involves asking if they have Braille menus—or my wife reads me the menu. I eventually decide on what I'd like to eat. Then, we wait for our waiter to come. Oftentimes, my wife will be asked, "Ma'am, what will you have?" After my wife gives her order, she is then asked, "Ma'am, what will he have?" My wife will then gesture for the individual to address me directly. "I don't know, what will he have?" I sometimes smirk and say, "Who knows what he will have?" shrugging and speaking sarcastically about myself in the third person. I can usually anticipate when this type of exchange will happen. I am good at knowing when people are giving me eye contact and giving each other eye contact. Initially, from the beginning, I sometimes get no eye contact or acknowledgement. My difference creates discomfort and avoidance of interacting with me.

What's for sure is that wherever I go, I am usually the "only one" like me. My blindness sets me apart, makes my world unlike that of others, and goes against the status quo. I am the "strange" character, the abnormal person, the frightening being. That sounds like a monster to me—or, if I don't qualify as a monster, I am, at times, treated like one. I feel like an ogre that has been granted limited permission to roam about the city among the masses, and my wife is treated as if she is my master, speaker, zookeeper, custodian, and handler. When I am released on the streets without a guardian, the crowd freezes.

"How come you are alone?"
"Don't you have someone to help you?"
"Isn't your wife afraid of you traveling the streets of Philadelphia by yourself?"
These are some of the comments I get from fellow pedestrians.

Countless sighted people tell me, time and time again, that if they were blind, they would give up. They would not leave their homes, they would not work, and consequently, they would stop living. I feel that many people are paralyzed by the dark, and in consequence, they try to paralyze me. To them, my safety is always an issue, so the best way to keep me safe is to cage me. "Stay home."

"Someone should be with you."
"I'm afraid you might get hit by a car."
"What if you get lost?"
"Better safe than sorry."

I would actually rather be sorry that I hadn't made an effort to responsibly live. Staying safely in a cage of darkness is not an option. Just the other day, a guy came up next to me on the street. I was walking down Walnut Street in Center City, Philadelphia. A set of footsteps emerged on my right, and a voice said, "Dude, I'm walking to your right. I wanted to just say something to you. I don't know how you can walk around the city and not see. I can't even get up at night to pee in my own house when it's dark at night. I'm totally scared." I thanked that guy very much for his candid and frank comments about my blindness. It was, first of all, refreshing for someone to speak to me openly about it; and secondly, for him to appreciate my skills. Sometimes, an angel will cross my path who understands that I am human, with thoughts, feelings, and motivations, but those interactions are rare.

Usually, the consistent reaction of others wears on me. Sometimes, I've felt so evil, as if I were a demon possessed, a rebellious fallen child of God. I've been in churches where I was asked, "What has your mother done to cause you to be blind?" I've come across irrational, unspiritual zealots who insist that my blindness is anything but a spiritual gift from God. Instead, they view it as a punishment for past sins. It's the manifestation of a blindness-causing demon, or a test of faith involving physical sight.

I remember an impactful experience I once had in church. When I was in college, I went to an old wrestling buddy's place of worship. Dontae and I had wrestled together at Central High School, and had become very close. He was an amazing teenager with an unyielding tenacity in life. Dontae was a courageous wrestler and a motivating friend; and later, he became a divinely inspired minister. While he was a minister-in-training, he asked me to come to his church. After high school wrestling, we searched for other connections in our friendship, and the main one was The Lord. He and I often talked about God, prayed together, and talked on the phone in an effort to continue our friendship. I ended up going to the church with him and another brother/high school friend of ours. Since Dontae was part of the pastoral team, he was behind the scenes when the church service started. It began with a praise-and-worship section filled with joyous, heartfelt, upbeat songs. I clapped my hands and sang. I could hear the organ up front, and a choir. The choir sounded like there were about 10 singers, but they didn't sound at all like a small group. They bellowed out verses and hymns. "Victory is mine! Victory is mine! Victory today is mine!" That song reminded me of my grandmother, who had been a lifelong church member and singer. She loved those "old-school songs" in her traditional black Baptist church. When I heard the song, I smiled, and continued to tap my feet and clap to the rhythm. After all, victory was mine! I was healthy, blessed with friends and family, and had been accorded an unwavering faith in God.

At some point during the praise and worship, the music came to a hush, and I felt a hand grab my left wrist. An older woman's voice from the front said, "Bring 'em up!" and Dontae's friend and a couple of other hands pushed me into the aisle and closer to the front of the church. Other hands pulled me closer to that woman's voice. It felt like five or six pairs of hands unapologetically clutching onto me. I wasn't sure what was going to happen. I had no idea. I felt a bit of reluctance, and stiffened. "What's going on?" For a moment, I hoped this was one of those "come close to the altar" moments for the entire church; but to my horror, it was only for me.

"Come out of him, Satan!" she said. Then I felt greasy, oily hands smack my forehead. "I said, come out of him!" Then my eyes were gouged, and my face was covered in oil. I smelled a fragrance like frankincense. She then kept her hands on me and commanded, "Fall back!" She was actually trying to get me to fall backward, but I guess I wasn't over-taken by a Godly spirit. She pushed my head back-wards, and my neck yielded as if I were looking up to the sky, or being force-fed poison. I was then dragged down to the ground by hands on my shoul-ders, upper back, and arms. On my back, I lay won-dering, "What the hell is going on here?"

"Repeat after me. Forgive me, Lord, for my sins!" her voice screeched. I repeated the forced confes-sional: "Forgive me, Lord, for my sins."

"In the name of Jesus, I rebuke you, Satan!" she instructed.

"In the name of Jesus, I rebuke you, Satan," I re-peated.

"Open your eyes," she then commanded. I tried, but by now, my eyes were stinging. I opened them, so she could see the eyes of this demonic monster. She then said, "I did all I could. There's nothing else I can do."

A hush came over the church. The music stopped, and the silence was piercing. What the hell just happened? I thought to myself. I was emotionally numb, and felt a distant rage from which I separat-ed myself in the moment. Hands then pulled me up, and I sat down in my seat in the pew. I couldn't be-lieve that I was the monster.

I'd never had an experience like that before. There had been hints by parishioners that I needed to have enough faith to get my eyesight back, and that I needed to pray more. Others insisted that God wanted me to see, and used biblical scripture to justify their biased conclusions. Some worshipers adamantly asserted that I could not serve God as a blind man, and that Jesus wants us to be whole— but I had never experienced an exorcism performed over me. I was humiliated. I felt belittled and dirty.

Maybe they are right. Maybe God has an issue with me, and it's my fault. Hell, no! They are fucking crazy. Why...how...could someone think that about me? I pushed those thoughts away quickly. Why hadn't I stopped this absurdity from happening? I knew that this was just downright uncomfortable and strange. The problem was, I was always taught to respect the elders and pastors of the church, and the godly. I had never had anyone talk to me about such a topic. No one had prepared me for the trauma I was facing in that moment. It was as if I had been a victim of a violent crime, and now I was thinking back to how I could have stopped it...or how I could have made sure that it never happened again.

I thought back to where my first messages about God had come from. They had come from my mother and my grandmother, who had never said anything like this to me about God, who God was, or what God thought about me. If God was punishing me, how come I didn't know what I had done wrong? If God was punishing my mother, how come He couldn't just punish her, and not me? Leave me out of it. If God wanted me to see, how come I was blind? And if it was my fault for not having enough faith, how much faith did I need to have? If I was demon possessed, how come I felt human?

My condition made sense in the material/scientific world. There was an actual, medical explanation for my blindness. I knew this, because I had 13 operations to account for it. I didn't think God was punishing me. I thought He had blessed me with life and happiness, and that life was full of imperfections. I thought my blindness was a part of me, and that my life could still go on—but there seemed to be a group of people who kept telling me, in one way or another, that I was flawed. I was abnormal. I was strange. I was far from pure. I was evil. I was a monster. Which one was it? Was I a child of God, as my mother had always taught me, or was I the shell of a demonic spirit or rebellious sinner?

When my mother, sister, and I went to church, it consisted of going into the building, sitting in a pew, and leaving immediately after the service was finished. We did not socialize, fraternize, or hobnob with anyone from the church. My mother tells me now that she was very sensitive about what people had to say. She even interpreted some looks from others as looks of disgust toward her for having a blind son. She was afraid of that probing, critical eye. She actually thought some people were skeptical of her and the way in which I had become blind. Before my mother had recommitted herself to a Baptist church, she had studied with the Jehovah's Witnesses for a two-year stretch in my childhood. She appreciated their attentiveness, their studiousness, and the fact that they came to you (in your home) instead of you going to them. That stretch overlapped the time period during which I was losing my eyesight. My mother started going to the Hall less and less in order to tend to my medical needs. An elder who was studying with her told her something that she will never forget. They said to her, "If you leave God, God will leave you." My mother was devastated. After this experience— coupled with other fundamental clashes—that particular stint was terminated. After hearing those hurtful words, she was haunted. At the time my mother needed God the most, spiritual people were telling her that He was not with her. As a consequence, she was very protective of me and our family in church. She wasn't going to let others inaccurately define our relationship with God.

Over the years, many people have tried to define my relationship with God according to my blindness, but many of them were—and still are—wrong.

I remember when I attended the University of Pittsburgh. I was the member of a couple of on-campus ministries. These clubs were great places to be in fellowship, and to be with others. Their intentions were always good. Meetings included a couple-dozen students getting together with a local minister to stand around holding hands, singing songs, and sharing in a common belief in Christ. All of us were eager yet naive students who prayed for all kinds of help: passing some midterm exam, family relationships, friendships, and romantic relationships. I remember being so nervous in these groups, at times. I often wanted to be a part of the group, but never really shouted and jumped up and down in the name of the Lord, so at times, I felt like a loner. Now, I know: it's not how loudly you shout, but how soft your heart is for God. I have always yearned to know truth, to seek out spiritual purpose in my life, and to please God.

One Friday afternoon, as I was walking through the lobby of the Towers dorms, I heard students talking, socializing, and roaming about their business; but as I walked closer to my dorm entrance, I heard a few people gathered in praise. Oh, listen—it was my buddies from the campus ministry. They were riled up and praising God. They loved me, and, of course, greeted me and let me know they were having a fellowship right there in the middle of campus. One brother excitedly said, "We were just praying that God would send us a sign, answer a prayer, or grant a miracle." Oh, no...whenever I heard "miracle" talk, I knew people were looking at me. Yikes. It was my time to "see!" They rushed over, pulled me to the center of their circle, their hands touching me with softness, yet passion. Another brother said, "Father God, we know you can do anything! Your words said that you gave sight to the blind, hearing to the deaf, and legs for the lame to walk! Yes, Lord...yes, Jesus..."

Oh, no, I know where this is going, I thought to myself. Even though I was doubtful that at this time, my sight would miraculously be restored, I prayed and acquiesced. Besides, if God wanted me to receive my sight, I'd be ready.

Well, needless to say, when we all opened our eyes, I was still blind. I mean, WE were all still blind. I couldn't see with my physical eyes, and they couldn't see with their spiritual eyes. I felt their hands let go of me, and they dispersed. I was alone. Wow. Had I disappointed them? Had God disappointed them? Had they disappointed me? Had God disappointed me? Was my doubt the reason that God hadn't made this miracle come true? I left the situation feeling uneasy and unsure about where God and I stood. I was convinced that I was blessed for my life, for the good fortune and opportunities I had received thus far, and for all I hoped for my life; but once again, people were telling me something different. I was unsure about where I stood with other Christians. Why was I the one who needed a miracle and some "fixing?" Why was I the one who was "suffering," even when I wasn't feeling any pain? I was the abnormal one, the weird creature, again—the monster.

From the age of nine, when I had started experiencing significant eye problems, up to my early adult years, I had met many demoralizing and frightening people; but God also put people in my life to teach me that I was, indeed, a creation of His with an eternal purpose. Thank God, I had people in my life who could see with their spiritual eyes. After losing my eyesight, I spent many hours listening to my radio, trying to learn anything and everything I could about God. I listened to a local radio show host, Louise Williams. Her voice would bellow out praises and worship to Jesus. It cracked and strained with passion and fervor: "Yes, Lord! Please bless us, Lord! We need you, God! Bring us closer to You, God! Touch us with your Holy Spirit. Draw us unto you." I did pray with her that God would bless me, and bring me closer to Him, and help me to know His purpose in my life and in my darkness.

Whenever I came home from college for winter, spring, or summer break, I visited my home church, Mount Carmel Baptist, where Pastor Albert Franklin Campbell led his flock. My mother, sister, and I had joined when I was about eleven years old, and I had always felt such love there—partly because it was very organized and structured, and low-key for a traditional Black church. I also felt safe, because my mother made sure that nobody said or did anything damaging to us. I can just imagine her stern voice saying, "Don't start none, won't be none." As a result, our participation was limited. Our hellos were quick, restrained, yet cordial; and our goodbyes were quicker, distant, and hurried. We were sure not to let anyone get too close.

One of the most impactful experiences I had in church was my baptism. On that occasion, my mother had to allow someone to get close to us. It was a warm June Wednesday night in 1988, when I was eleven years old. I remember it was a school night, and I had even told my teachers, Ms. Smith and Ms. Peters, that I would be up late at church getting baptized.

It was a wonderful evening. There was lots of singing, and people enthusiastically praying and talking. The energy in the church was electrifying. I could feel power stirring among the crowd. People got up one by one to become baptized. One would step down into the pool to be immersed into the water...or, more accurately, dunked. Pastor Campbell was very clear that we would not be sprinkled with water, merely dipped in the water, or splashed with water. We would be dunked completely down under the water, to rise up as a new being. Each of us was asked if we believed in Jesus Christ, if we believed He died for our sins, and if we believed He had risen from the dead. Then another hymn was sung, to get the next person prepared. I remember one woman panting, "YES, YES, YES!!! Yes, Lord, I do!" I could hear the urgency in her voice. She needed God with every ounce of her being. Everyone was excited. They believed that God was there, and that He was touching every newborn soul.

I remember when my turn came up. I stood in the pool next to my pastor. I felt his hands around me. He hovered over me, and I felt his body, his robe, and his arms envelop me. It was great. I felt so loved and cared for.

"Do you believe that Jesus Christ is Lord, and that He died and rose again for the forgiveness of your sins?" the pastor asked. I was nervous. I had heard some people say "I do," as if they were agreeing to marriage vows. I heard others say, "Yes," as if they were simply answering. I hesitated. "Yes, I do," I said, and the congregation echoed back to me:

"Amen."
"Praise the Lord."
"My, my."

The pastor put his hand over my mouth to make sure I didn't drown, and pushed me back; and then I was quickly brought back up. The singing continued. It was joyous! I don't remember what my thoughts were at that moment; I just remember my feelings. I felt so happy. I was crying, and kept crying. My mother was so happy.

One distinct memory I have about that moment was my grandfather hugging and kissing me all over my face after I had been baptized. He was so proud. It seemed like the music and the singing and the praises went on and on all night. Looking back, I know that I felt accepted, supported, and loved. I was a creation of God. I was not a monster. God even had a plan for me, and wanted to be close to me; and that night, I felt close to Him.

That pivotal moment in my spiritual and existential development reminds me of a song with which I had heard my grandmother humming along when we used to listen to the Hour of Power on Sunday nights on the radio. She attended Cornerstone Baptist Church during the day, and listened to services in the evening. One of my favorite songs was "Lord, I Lift My Spirit to You." The singers weren't great. They sounded like old women who were giving their last breath to sing for God. Their voices creaked like rusty doors, which didn't do much for their pitch. They sounded winded, as if they were in the midst of a hard workout. They were on the beat, though, and they sang with passion. They meant what they said. Those words came alive. Their hearts and souls merged with the music to make people cry and shout for joy. Their voices could break you down and have you sobbing at the undeniable feeling of God's presence. They lifted their spirits to His spirit. Their voices literally and figuratively strained to the heavens, to "touch the hem of His garment." I loved hearing that song.

> Lord, I lift my spirit,
> To Your spirit
> In holy sweet communion
> I sense Your holy presence
> As I draw nearer
> I lift my spirit, to You
>
> Lord, I give You glory
> I give You Honor
> You've given so much to me
> Your blood has saved me
> Your power has raised me
> To new life, new life, eternally
>
> Lord, You turned my sadness
> Into gladness
> You turned my confusion into joy
> And the peace You give me
> As You live in me
> The world has not destroyed.

Ms. Smith joked and said they saw wings and a halo over me when I fluttered into school the next morning. I was excited to be in a new community of believers, but I also had faith that God was with me and guiding me. Moreover, I was surrounded by people who believed in me. They believed in who I was, because I was a child of the Almighty Creator. I was His eternal creation.

Over the next decade, I had experiences with my pastor that affirmed who I was, and confirmed who I would later become. I remember sitting next to him during a service when I was around twelve years old. I was asked to do the call to worship for a Youth Sunday, and had the privilege of sitting next to him. Several times during the service, he kept bugging me by saying the same phrase over and over again. "Andre." "Yes, Pastor?" I replied.

"God bless you." I replied with a thank-you. Then, a minute later, he said, "God bless you," again, but this time with a strong emphasis on the bless you. He couldn't stop saying it over and over again. "Andre, God bless you;" and that time, the emphasis was on the word God. This went on at least a half-dozen times. What's this guy's deal? That's weird. I heard him the first time, and the second, and the third. Maybe he likes me, I kept thinking to myself.

It was simple, as I now know. He was praying that God would have favor upon me. He prayed for me often. He never said so outwardly, but I could tell in the way he spoke to me, touched me, and greeted me. I was a child of God. My pastor believed in me. He knew that God had something special for me, and he prayed that I would find that purpose. I am so thankful for him, and for his leadership and love over me. He didn't preach down to his congregation, crush us with fire-and-brimstone messages, or damn us to Hell. He explained the Bible, then walked the walk.

My relationship with my church, along with my grandmother and mother, planted seeds in me. I knew that if I drew close to God, He would meet me the rest of the way. If I just stretched my hands to Him and sought His holy presence, He would not forsake me. He would speak to me through life's experiences, and through His people. Coincidences were not just coincidences, but confirmations. More and more people started to give me credit and praise about who I was on the inside. I received this from my schoolteachers as well as my friends. They found me valuable, and believed that I could study and learn, and that I was good. I was a good soul.

As I have gained more and more steam throughout my spiritual walk as a blind man, I have come to believe that God has taught me life lessons "in the dark." Our thinking is backwards when it comes to seeing. Jesus says in John 20:29, "Because you have seen Me, you have believed. Those who believe without seeing are blessed" (Holman Christian Standard Bible, 2015). I believe that this passage highlights the way in which people remain fixated on sight and physical proof. They seem to need concrete certainty. Faith is too hard if there's risk involved. Faith is often associated with blindness; and faith is terrifying, because you cannot see where you're going or evidence for what you believe. We are consumed with what we can see. Instead of living life to build our character, take risks, and step out on courage, we need to know that everything we do will have a positive, "for-sure" outcome.

We have lots of work to do if we expect to "see" everything in life. For example, we cannot see the future. As a result, people are afraid about what will happen tomorrow, what will happen at their job, what will happen in their relationships, what will happen in their marriages, what will happen to their children, and what will happen in their lives.

There are many unanswered questions in life. This is inevitable. We are in the dark. We don't know what the future holds, or what to expect. As life goes on, challenges arise that force us to take chances on education, careers, jobs, each other, our children, and ourselves. The most frustrating thing about being a therapist is working with someone who cannot see their true potential. They are paralyzed by the fear of what they cannot see, both in the future and in their lives. The future is the dark, and looking forward is unsettling and distressing.

God builds our faith by allowing situations to happen to us when we can't see. As a result, we have to follow Him. When I first lost my eyesight, my mother and I tried to find ways to navigate outside. I mostly held onto her arm and followed her lead. I could not see where we were going. I did not know what was ahead of us, and I had to trust her. She could have walked me off a cliff or into a river, but she didn't, of course; I'm here telling this story. When we first went out, she would tell me, "Now, we're coming to some steps," and I knew steps were coming. Other times, she said to me, "You have to jump over a puddle," and I jumped when she said go. By the way, she knew that just because I was blind, that didn't mean I couldn't take leaps of faith. Other times, she would say, "We need to speed up," and I would step up my pace. Sometimes, I didn't have the benefit of hearing clear directions from her, and we took a few risks. For example, when we would go to the supermarket, we walked a few blocks, and she had to pull our shopping cart. The sidewalk was too narrow for me, her, and the cart. Instead of walking beside her, I had to follow her. She would dangle her keys in her hand, and I would follow the sound and walk with my white cane. When we were going straight, I kept straight; when it was time to curve to the right, I heard the keys, and followed; and when she stopped, I put on the brakes. If we were in a rush, she couldn't always tell me when there would be a step up or down, or to speed up or to slow down. Instead, I had to be syn-chronized with the feeling of her arm and body, or the sound of her footsteps. Eventually, I learned to navigate the paths my mother and I walked on my own. I learned to trust, to follow, to listen, to feel,

and then to do. All of this came about without physically seeing where to go.

My courage, emotional strength, and confidence
were getting built up more and more strongly.
When I walked off the path, I did not stop; I kept going. I kept listening, feeling, and walking. God teaches us how to live our lives in the same way. We need
to follow His directions, listen to His voice, feel for
His push and pull, and then, finally, do what He has
put us on earth to do. This builds trust. Then we are
believing in God, in a divine purpose in our lives,
and a reason for living. Now, "seeing is not believing," but "believing is seeing." Seeing potential in
self and others takes guts. Taking risks to be excellent, to be good, and to be all you can be takes faith.
It takes believing in what you cannot yet see, but
what you can already visualize, hear, and feel.

Monsters roam about without a godly purpose. In
many ways, monsters are freaks of nature, or exper-
iments gone wrong. They are accidents. Creations of
God are divine, orchestrated, and perfectly placed.
My life and my blindness were perfectly orchestrated so that I could be blessed. As a psychologist, I
have witnessed many people who needed someone
to help them in order to get the blessings life had
waiting for them, but they couldn't see. I help people go into the dark, search for their purpose, and
strive for clarity. That always takes hard work. They
don't know how long it will take, what the outcome

will be, or what will happen in their lives. I walk with them. They are often paralyzed with fear, and constrained by the demons of their past. Generational curses often haunt families, because they don't see it; or if they do see it, they can't see any other way to do things differently.

I help people to see from all different perspectives—and that is not easy. Many don't want to see the dark places in their souls. It's tough to look at yourself in the mirror. It's tough to see the mistakes of the past, and it's even scary to consider a wonderful possibility. It requires us to strive and stretch for God in order to get answers about our existence. Can you stretch for Him? When you can't see your way, are you listening for His voice? When life is uncertain, murky, and cloudy, can you still see Him? Are you begging that he reveal himself to you, so that you can see Him? Are you confused about your life? Are you drawing nearer to Him, so that He can show Himself to you? Do you feel like you're in the dark?

My grandmother's patient, humming voice comes back to me. She is humming the melody of "Lord, I Lift My Spirit to You."

Lord, You turned my sadness
Into gladness
You turned my confusion
Into joy

And the peace You give me
As You live in me
The world
Has not destroyed.

Lord, I lift my spirit,
To Your spirit
In precious sweet communion
I sense Your holy presence
As I draw nearer
I lift my spirit, to You
To You, to You, I lift my spirit, to You.

CHAPTER 3

Learning in the Dark

O ne of the best parts of being a child is having permission to dream. Children often fantasize about what they want to be when they grow up. They imagine the mansions they will live in, or whom they will marry. Some pretend to fight crime, do the impossible, or become inventors. I loved to think about all of the possibilities for what I could be when I grew up.

Up until the age of nine, the world was my oyster, something I could possess. Pretend play was the vehicle that took me on unforgettable journeys. My imagination was a horse running wild. Just before I lost my eyesight, my imagination was soaring at Commodore John Barry Elementary School in West Philadelphia, where I attended second and third grades. I remember pretending to be one of G.I. Joe's star characters, Flint, turning my hat to the side like a beret, and running wildly around the concrete playground jungle. At other times, I tried to bob and weave, using my lunch pail as a football, outmaneuvering my peers and leaving them in my wake—at least that's what my imagination would have me believe. In other moments, I made believe I was a Michael Jackson lookalike by taking off one glove, moonwalking, and kicking my leg. Other days, I was a movie star in the latest breakdancing movie: gesticulating, pop-locking, spinning on my back, and wiggling my little body like a snake. Sometimes, my wild horse of an imagination went too crazy. Once, I wished I was a superhero, jumped off bricks that were a couple of feet off the ground, with arms stretched out and legs kicked back, and I landed flat on my face. I spent a few minutes gasping for air, holding my chest, and wishing I had never dared to fly.

When adults asked me what I wanted to be when I grew up, I responded like a kid who had been well-coached: "A doctor, a lawyer, a judge, a policeman, or a fireman." My mother took careers and education seriously, and made sure I was always looking to "be somebody" when I grew up. Because she was a teacher, she imprinted onto my impressionable brain the importance of education. She used to sit down with me and make sure I got my work done. Misbehavior was not tolerated. Respect for adults was not a choice—it was required. Those precious people—teachers, educators, and dreamcatchers—were viewed as helpers and gatekeepers of knowledge and opportunity. They were to be revered and highly esteemed.

Previous to school at Barry, I had extraordinary experiences going to kindergarten in Germany and first grade in Texas. My stepfather was in the army, and it gave us opportunities to travel when I was between the ages of four and seven. Living in Germany for two years, I discovered languages. I often played with German children who didn't speak English, but that didn't matter. We found ways to play in a sandbox, run around after each other, or make a snowman without any way to communicate in the same language. Cultural differences were not important to us. In my kindergarten class, the class of American army kids often played games and had fun with the German kids. I was so interested in knowing what they were thinking or saying. It's amazing how children are so innately able to make connections with others. Their openness, flexibility, and curiosity make every child prime for emotional learning.

After we returned to the States, we lived in Texas, where I attended the first grade. Even though these children all spoke English, I often felt alone and different. See, I was the only black face in that room. I remember it being obvious to me on my first day, in the room of cute, young, white faces. I felt like something was different, but I didn't know what. It was ironic that I was with a group of teachers and classmates who spoke the same language as I did, but I still felt like a foreigner.

My mother admits now that she thought my teacher may have been biased against me for being the only black boy. I don't remember why, but I sat in the corner in my class. I was teased, and didn't feel like I had any friends.

I was even paddled once for going out to play without completing my morning schoolwork. When we finished copying the poem of the day, practicing letters, and counting numbers by two, five, and ten, we were allowed to go out to recess; but if we did not finish, we had to stay in. I had partially completed it, handed in the work, and given it to my teacher. A paddling with a wooden paddle was the punishment for my crime. Nowadays, this in itself is considered a crime. It was actually was not illegal then, because in 1983, this kind of corporal punishment was allowed in schools. Today, it would be an automatic lawsuit.

I was so ashamed to be paddled in front of the class. There was actually another kid in my class, a white little boy who used to get paddled every single day. I felt so badly for him. Not only did he sit in a corner, but his desk was placed in a huge box. It was like a doghouse keeping him in there. The things that teachers got away with in the 80s were outrageous.

At the end of that school year, my first-grade teacher in Texas told my mother, either through

grades or an unofficial assessment, that I should repeat the first grade. My mother responded with, "Oh
no, he doesn't." She would not have her son repeat-
ing a grade. I'm not sure how—maybe it was by
sheer will—but she was able to convince teachers
back in Philadelphia that I was capable of continu-
ing on to the second grade. We returned to Philadelphia, and that's when I started at Barry.

My first classroom experience at Commodore
John Barry Elementary was similar, but different.
This time, I sat down in a classroom of all black faces. My teachers were also black. I enjoyed my education there. I had so much fun with the other little
black boys as we played together, got to know each
other so well, and felt protective of one other. There
was a camaraderie between us. We understood one
another. We were like an army of soldiers, a team of
players, a group of friends. My education didn't
mean much to me; my friends were most important.
The power that we felt in our group was exhilarating. I belonged, and felt at home at Barry—and then,
I started having problems with my eyesight.

I missed quite a bit of school in the third grade
because of operations and recovery times. In those
days, surgeries to reattach a detached retina were
invasive, intrusive, and painful to the patient's eye. I
spent days in the hospital recovering, then days at
home. I was unable to open my swollen, gooey,
goopy, eyelids for days, and even after I was able to

open them, my eye was sore and very tender to the touch. It rolled around to the back of my head whenever I had another excruciating round of eye drops, at least four to six times a day. I had to wear a plastic shield to protect my eye, because a breeze literally sent me gasping for air out of pain. My eyeball stung, throbbed, and watered profusely. Bending over and participating in contact sports was forbidden, as any sudden motion or knocks against my head, eye, or face could cause my retina to redetach.

At the beginning of the fourth grade, I was not even able to start school. I had undergone surgery toward the end of the summer, and never got to start fourth grade. I was given a homebound teacher. It was at this time that I started to need a reader and someone to help me with my work. I needed to sit closer to the television set, change the contrast of the colors in order to see it, and get up real close to see a face. My vision was good enough to see general shapes. The details of people, places, and things, though, were sometimes impossible. I hoped that the vision that I once had would resurrect itself, and help me to see what was around me. Small print on a newspaper or textbook was almost impossible. I used to like to open up Jet magazines to "read the articles" about the swimsuits—well, at least, that's what I told my mother when she caught me once. Thankfully, I was still able to see those swimsuits when I initially experienced eye problems—but not for long. I remember sitting in my grandmother's living room, trying to look at a newspaper to read the comics and scan through the TV guide. The lettering was distant, strange, and foreign. It was small. I could not make out words. I was shocked; it was fuzzy and blurry. This was a turning point in the gradual decline of my vision. My world was slowly changing.

After I had stayed home for the first two months of the fourth grade, my mother was told about the Overbrook Educational Center. OEC was a Philadelphia public school housed on the campus of the Overbrook School for the Blind. This was when the worst and the best things began happening to me at the same time. On the one hand, I was going blind; but on the other hand, my education would expand tremendously.

It was absolutely grueling to be homebound. Oh, how I missed my friends at Barry. I cried many days, because I hated being at home. I should have been outside running and jumping and dancing, but instead, I was told that I should be safe. I wasn't allowed by my grandmother to go outside and play. It was too risky. Being homeschooled was excruciating. Watching television was all I had to do. I watched every episode of *The Price Is Right*. I became good at guessing the numbers, and wished that I could win $10,000 in a game in which contestants spun a huge wheel. I watched the talk show host Phil Donahue, and had no idea what he was talking about. I just remember hearing the word "sex," and that people responded with such excitement. I even got into a soap opera called The Young and the Restless, and became familiar with the characters and themes. There was lots of talk about this "sex" stuff there, too. As exciting as staying home from school might sound, it was nothing like that. I missed my friends so much.

I just knew there had to be a way to contact one of them. How could I do it? I actually found out about something called "information," or directory assistance, and called for "Dana Persons," my good friend from the third grade. He lived on Race Street, a half a block away from Barry. "Can I have the phone number for my friend Dana Persons, who lives at 59th and Race?" There was a pause on the phone from a nasal, robotic human voice. "Hold, please. Your number is ..." And guess what? I got a telephone number, and I called him. Oh, how I missed him so much—but just hearing his voice and talking with him about what was going on at Barry was exciting. We chatted about teachers, sports, and girls. He and I are still great friends today, as adults.

When I started at OEC, I was excited to get my education going, and to meet new friends. Life at OEC was much different from Barry. There were no walls full of artistic graffiti; instead, there were acres of trees, greenery, and plants. My class shrunk down from 30 students to less than 10. All of us were visually impaired. Recess involved some of the totally blind kids standing over by a wall, talking and making silly noises, or going up and down the sliding board. The visually impaired children integrated with the sighted children at lunch, and played kickball or swung on swings. The teachers were just as nice and caring, but they seemed a little more patient, and since I was in a smaller classroom setting, they probably had a little more energy, as well.

Now, I had more chances of getting help with my work, and I was really held accountable. These teachers expected work out of me, even though I was losing my eyesight. After a month at OEC, my fourth-grade teacher, Mrs. Ruffo, made the decision with my mother to put Braille and white-cane instruction into my educational plan. My vision was low, I was now using a pair of incredibly thick glasses, and the stability of my retinas was unknown. Learning skills around reading and safe travel were now at the top of the list. Before this experience, play was important: now, work was more important.

At OEC, I noticed that the kids were different. First, they read and wrote in another way. Some students read large print with their eyes. Carnell, Elijah, and Yolanda all read large print. They stammered through words just like any "typical" child, but they had an even heartier determination to read, even though they were sometimes struggling, losing their place, or snailing along. I did try to read large print, but that was even more frustrating. My vision had decreased to the point where reading with my very thick glasses was ineffective. We even tried using a closed-circuit television system. With the CCTV, as it was called, I placed books and papers under a camera, and it blew up the letters on a screen. That worked some, but it was so slow. It took forever to read a line of text, or to write something. It took coordination to work the CCTV, write, read, and then finally process the actual work. Braille was the best option for me. It allowed me to struggle less to use my eyes, and to use my hands, instead. The hope was that once I was fluent in Braille, I would then be able to focus on my work.

I started to learn Braille with my dear Braille teacher, Mrs. Bassett. She was elegant, very tall, and slender, and spoke in a slow, classy voice. "Honey," (she dragged the word out to three syllables), "We're going to learn Braille, and you'll like it, honey." She read Braille fast and without error. Wow, she was amazing. I learned Braille, and it was not easy.

Braille is another language of its own. It is a six-dot system that comes from Morse code. Varying combinations of dots equal different letters, numbers, symbols, and words. I remember trying to read those miniature, teeny-tiny dots. They were so small. I couldn't tell one letter from the other. My teacher started me off with the alphabet, but man, did it take forever—and every day, she introduced something new. It was a slow process, but she made it go so fast. I actually had to press on the letters extra-hard so I could decipher the different patterns. My fingers had not developed the sensitivity that they currently possess. They were sore, and they ached. I often found myself sleepy after struggling to read, because it was so painstakingly slow. Misreading one dot could screw up the entire meaning of a whole sentence. At times, I lost interest, made faces at my teacher who couldn't see me, and even clowned around by putting some of the Braille tools in my mouth. Every day required that I pay attention and work, but like any child, I was off-task at times. It was a slow and arduous process. Thankfully, there were other kids in that class who were blind and read very well. They were my role models.

I remember hearing one kid named David read. It was slow, but smooth and interesting. Donald read, too, with persistence and confidence. Christy and April always seemed to have a smile on their faces when they read. These kids were doing this Braille/blind thing, and seemed just fine academically—and what was striking was that they were happy, too.

Education at OEC was first-class. The principal, Mrs. Marilyn Moller, was also visually impaired, and expected excellence out of her teachers and students. She believed in all of us, no matter what our visual acuity happened to be. We had a monthly writing contest in which the principal read every single paper of every single student in the school, kindergarten through eighth grade. She was then able to see the educational talent of every student, and the teaching effectiveness of all of the teachers. I remember my first writing assignment, which I completed by recording my voice. I did not know Braille well enough yet, and could not yet type on a typewriter. My vision was no longer sufficient for writing. As a result, I spoke on tape—about Harriet Tubman. I was shocked to win first place for that report.

A lot of the work I did, I did on my own, but lots I did with the help of my mother and my cousin Zina Johnson. My mother found my new world to be perplexing. One time, my mother and I spent hours on trying to find the right page for my math assignment in a braille book. Other times, I struggled with just figuring out if I was reading upside down or not. This was one situation that my mother couldn't yell or coach her way through. She tried though. Once, we were up for what seemed like all night doing multiplication problems. It required that I multiply big numbers like 4,321 times 5,6789. My mother would check it and that night, it seemed like

I couldn't get any problem right. My mother got so upset with me, she started yelling and berating me for how I did not know what I was doing. I got another problem wrong, then another, and then another. She was slowly growing in impatience and frustration. Her yelling, her sighs, and comments got so loud and intense. She was enraged. I now know that she was feeling the pain and sadness of a parent of a blind child. She was not in my world, and she had no idea how I could "see." She was beside herself. "You'll never get this!" she yelled. Then, she stopped, paused, and asked me in a softer tone, "Wait, what was your answer?" I gave it to her. Then, she said, "What was your answer for the previous one?" I told her that answer as well. She then softened, came over to me, and hugged me. She said she had been doing the problems wrong herself on the calculator where she was checking my work and I was indeed getting the problems correct. Nights like these were not every night, but just one was too much to stomach.

So, Mom turned my education for a period of time over to an older cousin of mine, Zina. Zina was known as the smart one in my family as she had me by 4 years and attended The Illustrious Philadelphia High School for girls. Zina was absolutely beautiful with sweet patience and a quick mind. She never yelled or became fussy with me. She actually seemed to like tutoring me every Saturday. She liked it so much, she decided to have me teach her braille. Before I knew it, she was playing on my braille typewriter and reading my book reports. She believed in me as well, and even though she did not know much about blindness, she was smart and had an open mind to learn. Zina helped me with math, book reports, reading, and even practicing my braille. My mother still supported me, but mostly stuck to reading books on tape for me that were not in braille. God sent her to us. What a blessing she was.

As I progressed at OEC, I became more and more confident in my special blindness skills and academic skills. By the time I reached the 6th grade, I had lost all of the vision with which I was born in this world, and was getting ready to embark upon a life of a totally blind person, in the dark. I was not sure what I wanted to be at this point. My days at Barry School in West Philly were faint memories. The fantasies and dreams of being a soldier were fading, and my hopes to become a doctor were also in doubt. Playing football was impossible. What was I going to do with my life? I was not sure—but what I did know was that the same person I was as a sighted kid was the same kid I was as a blind kid. All of a sudden, when the conversation came up between my mother and others, she heard hesitation and uncertainty. I was no longer given a chance. I was made into a charity. One of her colleagues, a math teacher, told her with confidence, "There's no way he'll be able to do advanced math like algebra or geometry." I later found out that the reason I had had the same Spanish instructor throughout high school was because no other teacher was confident enough to teach me. When I told a camp counselor that I was thinking about becoming a psychologist, he was boldly doubtful that my aspirations were realistic: "You won't be able to see your patients." From an early time in my blindness, I received all sorts of messages about can't. You can't do this, and you can't do that were far too common—for me or for any child's experience. It was abusive. Every child needs to know that they can do anything, if they believe they can and work hard enough to achieve it. Because I had been sighted at one time, I was in on the secret. That secret was that sighted children got many more encouraging statements than blind kids.

Thank God, others believed in me. I needed someone to tell me that I could do something with my life—and be good at it! Not only did they tell me that I could do something good with my life, they also let me know that I could be better at it than others. I did take math up to calculus, and was actually tutored by a blind mathematician, Mrs. Mason. It was amazing that she could understand so much, remember so many numbers in her head, and do the problems so effortlessly.

My mother's voice still echoes in my head as I reflect today. My mother pushed me to be the best.

She knew that it was not for mere bragging rights or arrogant strutting, but that it was absolutely, unequivocally necessary that I be better than others just to have a chance to be considered. Just to be considered for a prestigious position or an excellent opportunity, I would have to outshine everyone else convincingly.

From my sixth-grade year on up, I was on a tear through academics. I made honor roll after honor roll, and won academic award after academic award. By the time I reached the eighth grade, it was time to determine which high school I would attend. After a lot of debate between my mother and teachers, we decided to apply to Central High School. Central was known for its academic vigor and competitive spirit. At first, my mother was doubtful, because it was far from my home, and I would have to take public transportation by myself. Ms. Moller pushed my mother to allow me to apply to Central. She wrote me one of the best letters of recommendation I ever received, and referred me as the best student she had seen in that decade.

While at OEC, I became well-adjusted. I learned Braille, how to type on a typewriter at a steady pace, and how to use a white cane in order to be independent. This was an exhilarating challenge. Mr. Foreman was my orientation and mobility instructor. Essentially, he taught me how to find my way. I learned compass directions, how to locate objects in space, how to use a cane on stairs and on the streets of Philadelphia, and how to travel safely.

I loved crossing streets the most. I used to come home when I was twelve years old and brag to my mother about my adventures with a cane. "Mom, you should have seen me today. I crossed a busy street. A car turned in front of me and in back of me at the same time!" She was terrified. "What!?" My mother approached my mobility instructor, and asked him about what he was doing with me. She was not very happy to know that my life was in danger. I never thought it was. He taught me how to locate curves, poles, and other objects with my cane. Mr. Foreman also taught me to read traffic with my ears instead of my eyes. When I approached an intersection, I could determine whether it was stationed with a stoplight or a stop sign. I was also taught to listen to parallel traffic at my right or left shoulder, to know when a fresh green light came. I learned how to make sure I was walking in a straight line by lining up with that parallel traffic. Most people have no idea how the blind cross streets independently. They cannot imagine what it feels like. I was never terrified or scared. I definitely respected traffic, but always knew that if I had the skills, I could do it.

When I went to high school, I traveled across the city by myself. My mother made me call her daily from a payphone to let her know that I had arrived.

She got me extra training with Ms. Beth Levinbach, who was excellent—not only in her teaching, but also in helping my mother to relax. Beth would say, "Gladys, relax. He's going to be okay." Ms. Levinbach had a great raised-line drawing kit, which could be used to draw maps and sketch routes with raised lines that I could feel. That was cool. Many of my geometry books, geography books, and maps in school were designed with a similar technology, so I wouldn't be "in the dark."

At Central, I met some really smart students, but they weren't the best. The best students were the ones who put in time to be great. I will never forget two specific incidents. During my freshman year, I sat next to a young lady in biology class who was quiet, but very attentive. Her name was Tolin. I talked to her from time to time, and found out that her family was from Vietnam, and that she was the first generation to grow up in the United States. She got excellent grades, and scored higher than me on tests every time. I asked her, "What do you do to study?" She replied, "I read the chapters three times the night before the test." I was dumbfounded and astonished. She was not just "smart." She actually put in the time to be successful.

I also remember a tough guy, who studied all the time. He was a no-nonsense type of person, and I remember asking him the wrong question. "Hey, David, why do you study all the time here? Take it easy on chemistry." Without giving me time to close my mouth after my question, he quickly retorted, "What do you have in chemistry?" At that time, I had a C, and had struggled for the first half of the year. I replied, "A C." He said, "I have an A." That was it—he had nothing more to say. He had put in the time to get the results he wanted, and he definitely did not consider my blindness to be a copout.

I learned from Tolin and David that if I wanted anything in life, I would have to work hard for it— over and above anything else. There could be no easy ways out, shortcuts, or slacking. If I wanted to do well on a test, I had to study hard every day. I had to stay up late, and deny myself a movie and videogames. My education had to be something I would die for. I often thought of the black slaves, who had died for trying to read and write. I thought of their struggles, and how they had died in order for me to be able to have an opportunity to live life to the fullest.

When I traveled to Central, it took me over an hour. My mother did not allow me to take the subway, because she was afraid for my safety. From the beginning, I was starting to learn that I had to work harder than everyone else—even before I stepped into the school. I was up earlier, and I got home later. It took me longer to complete homework, and it took me longer to master the material—but through all of these tough experiences, I never used them for an excuse, because I was happy to be part of the crowd. I was not pushed into a corner and told to sit and be safe. I was told, "Do it!" And I did, with every fiber of my being.

As if traveling from West Philadelphia to North Philadelphia wasn't enough for my mother, I decided to go to the University of Pittsburgh for college. I majored in psychology and minored in Africana studies and Spanish.

During my senior year in high school, I'd had a conversation with the mother of a classmate. "What do you think you want to do in college?" she asked.

"I want to study psychology, Ma'am," I replied.

"Are you sure you can handle that? That's a lot of reading, I've heard." I'm sure she didn't even know how I'd gotten through high school, and the thought of me going through college was probably even more puzzling. I had shelves and shelves of Braille books at school, along with a Braille typewriter, which was incredibly heavy to carry around, and an endless number of books on tape. Tapes were everywhere in my bedroom: under the bed, in the closet, behind my dresser, and on top of my TV set. I was buried by them. I also used a laptop computer and a specialized tablet for blind students. I was able to take notes and listen to them in an earphone.

My typing teacher's instruction came in handy. During my first year in college, some great technology had just been released that allowed me to scan typed material so my computer could read it to me in a computerized voice. Before the days of scanning, blind college students had hundreds of tapes of books, and spent countless hours with readers. I had the good fortune of being able to be more independent—but even with the technological advances, I was still putting in much more time than other students. Scanning every page of every book that was not offered on tape from the Library for the Blind took forever. I scanned books for hours and hours.

The disability supports office at Pitt started scanning my work for me. I felt I was now living the easy life. I listened to my work at anywhere from 350 to 450 words a minute, depending upon the subject. I had to find my way around campus, and I did that primarily with another mobility instructor, at first. Getting lost on campus was not abnormal. When I did, I just relaxed, and tried to imagine in my mind's eye where I was, working myself toward where I needed to go. There was usually some cool cat or pretty girl who was willing to help. In this way, I met friends around campus—and some good helpers when I got into trouble.

When I graduated from college, I had hopes of going to graduate school for psychology. I had to take the Graduate Record Examinations and score well in order to give myself a chance. The only problem was that there were no talking computers at these testing sites, so I had to depend upon a reader for the test. I also received twice as much time because of the alternative format. Even though that accommodation was necessary, it just drew out the torture of sitting with some untrained reader. I remember when I took the exams for the first time, the person didn't know how to pronounce the word miserly, and pronounced it with a short i. I kept asking her over and over again to say that word, and it wasn't until I asked for the spelling that I got it. I also had to tell her to slow down when she was reading too fast, and speed up when she was going to slowly. It was agonizing and exhausting just to coach someone in how to help me. For a large part of that exam, I adjusted to the test reader instead of helping them adjust to me. Taking the test was stressful enough.

I didn't do well. I still applied to Widener, and hoped for the best. Widener University had a reputation as a great school for clinical psychology, and after some research, I decided to apply there. I was interviewed, and felt I did well. The interviewer did say, "I'm looking at the verbal section of your GREs. The score is, um, a little low. You seem like a pretty articulate guy. What happened?" I wasn't sure how to answer. I shrugged. I remembered that I had done better than average on the math section. Looking back, that was because it's a lot easier to read a math problem than a five-paragraph section with questions.

About two weeks after that interview, I received a call. "Andre, it looks like we won't be able to accept you," the professor said hesitantly. "Your scores on the verbal section of the GRE are low, and our program is unsure of how we would go about tailoring our curriculum to meet your needs as a visually impaired student." I hit the roof! I told him that this was very frustrating, and that I could handle anything that came my way. He was apologetic, and told me to raise my scores so the university could consider me again.

The next year, I studied for the GREs like a wild man. I got tapes on improving my vocabulary and increasing my understanding of the English language. I practiced using these words, and made Braille flashcards. I was telling people to throw any words at me, so I could try to figure out what they meant. I also practiced with a coworker of mine, Mark. Mark and I had met at a training program for the disabled. He was an instructor at a program that had asked me to be involved in doing some pseudo-career counseling with the other disabled people there. I was the only college graduate, and they were interested in me sharing my experiences with the other students who were visually impaired, hearing impaired, intellectually disabled, or affected by some other physical disability. In our off time,

Mark and I practiced. He read the questions and answers to me, then noticed something very interesting. "Andre, you're just listening to me. Interrupt me, tell me to speed up, slow down, and spell words. You need to take control and be boss of this exam." That was the best advice he could have given me; he had told me, essentially, to take the bull by the horns. I started excelling from that point forward. I needed to be obsessive, controlling, and hyper-vigilant for any problems with the reader, and gain as much clarity as possible about anything they said.

When the day of the test came, I was a bossy thorn in that reader's side. I made her spell words I didn't know, and speed up, slow down, go back, skip forward—even read something two or three times at super speed to make sure my answers were correct. My results came in a month later, and it turned out I had raised my score 25% on the verbal section and 20% on the mathematics section. I then set out to apply to Widener for the next year. When I was interviewed, a different professor said to me, "Any idea what I'm going to ask you?" I did not know, and I said something about the weather. He said, "No. How did you raise your score?" He knew of my prior year's rejection, and congratulated me on my hard work. I beamed with pride. Needless to say, I made it into graduate school to become a Doctor of Psychology.

The road through graduate school was tough, but the toughest tests were literally behind me. First, I had to learn the skills to be able to function in a world that was not designed for me. So many people feel like outcasts and outsiders, and excelling in a foreign place can seem impossible. Sometimes, you have to learn a new language, a new way of relating, or a skill that is by no means innate. At other times, you will be the only one like yourself, but that has to be blocked out mentally, with the goal of succeeding staying foremost in one's mind. I had to focus, and shut out all other distractions. Sometimes, that meant ignoring the negative doubts of others, and turning up the emotional volume of the voices that believed in me. I've always felt that in order to reach any goal, whether it be academic, financial, or personal, one has to stick to one's commitments. Finishing graduate school and becoming a psychologist was partly about my intellectual skill, but it was more about stick-to-itiveness, determination, and passion. I had to want to succeed more than anything else in the world.

When I found out that I had been accepted into graduate school, I was eating, and accidently knocked my plate onto the floor while jumping up and down. My passion was relentless, undying, and unwavering. I wanted it! In life, there are times when it's not about if you will succeed, but how you will succeed. I already knew that I was going to fight with everything I had to achieve my goals. To succeed, I needed to study two and three times as long as others, put aside frustration about my blindness, and keep moving forward. At times, I was almost on autopilot. It's similar to running a race or participating in an exercise. After you reach a certain point of fatigue, you will hit a zone, and your body will keep pumping, even when you want to stop. I was a robot, at times—and I became like steel. I made up my mind about what I was going to do, and I didn't listen to anyone else. After it was confirmed by others and by God that I was to be a psychologist, I never looked back.

In my practice, I have seen a number of visually impaired patients. One of my favorites, who I mentioned earlier in this text, was an older woman who was mildly intellectually disabled. As I got to know her, I found out that not only was she limited intellectually, but she also had low vision, and had actually benefited from special instruction in a school for the blind. We worked together on her relationships with her peers, her issues with her family, and her talents as an artist and singer. She was often asked to sing at weddings at her church, and boy, did she do that well. She actually sang for me the first time we met, and her strong, raspy, passionate voice filled my office. Her vibrato moved me with a feeling that cut to my soul, as she emotionally teleported me to a time long ago when black folks took in Negro spirituals for food and nourishment. Her voice filled my heart, just as it filled the space within the four walls of my office; I overflowed with emotion. She sang with a fervor you couldn't help but feel. The volume and unapologetic zeal in her voice moved me to the core, but of course, since I was seeing her for the first time, I chose to keep my reactions reserved for the sake of her treatment. I was forced to keep my "black church amens" to my-self, and smile in seemingly faint amusement.

Many times, she talked about how difficult it was for her to see, and how she often told people that she could not read because of her eyesight. She avoided having to read at her church or at restau-rants. After one of our sessions, I had her sign an important treatment plan document, and she was able to see it, but it was difficult for her to read it. I slowly realized that she was a complicated woman with learning difficulties and visual limitations. Her eye problems shook her confidence. "People treat me differently, Dr. Watson. You know when people talk to you…" she paused, "…they do this thing." She started to stutter. "They do this thing, I mean, they talk to me like, like I don't know anything," she con-tinued, and her voice grew in intensity. "They talk to me like I'm slow or something." I understood her pain. She was incredibly complex, and so tricky to understand. On the one hand, she had this eye prob-lem that she often told others about. It was what she told others in order to explain why she couldn't read well. Unbeknownst to her friends, she also had some intellectual challenges, but what was certain about her was her ability to touch people's hearts. I met her adult son once while we were working together, and he told me, "Doc, she has people in that church on their feet. She knows when to turn it on and when to turn it up!" Mary was skilled at feeling other people's emotions, and knowing what they needed and how they needed it through her singing. The call-and-response that is so common in many black churches was a language she understood so well. Her learning was emotional.

Mary's ability to understand emotions was why she did well in treatment. She started dating, leading a Bible study at her church, and even going on trips. She also began repairing her relationship with her son by talking with him more about her limitations. She was smart, but a different kind of smart. She was adaptable, and in some crucial moments, she was emotionally connected with people.

I remember a time when she connected with me. I had, of course, been having a tough time with previous patients who had so many questions about my blindness and their concerns about my ability to help; but Mary must have been able to read my emotions and what I needed to hear at that session. "Dr. Watson, I've learned so much from you," she confessed to me. "I mean, you are visually handicapped like me, and before I knew you, I thought I had an eye problem—but I now know it is an IQ problem. I don't learn things as fast as other people." Mary continued, "It's not eyesight that is important, but insight." I was torn. I was sad for her, as she was accepting some of her own limitations. On the other hand, I was proud that someone had actually acknowledged my own intellectual abilities. And it was at that moment that it occurred to me: Mary's weakness was also her strength. Her challenges with understanding math or reading gave her room to excel in other ways. She had become good at making connections with people. Yes, she did have an eye problem and an IQ problem—but she was developing emotional intelligence. Through her courage and her candid confession, she was actually showing her wisdom. William Shakespeare said, "The fool doth think he is wise, but the wise man knows himself to be a fool." The humility she exercised in life was the reason why she was so smart—and in so many ways.

Many times, we are so focused on what we cannot do in life. One person cannot see, another cannot hear, and another cannot walk; but in those weaknesses, strengths are born. For Mary, and also for me, visual impairment was the reason we had both been singled out and doubted. Mary had received a double dose of doubt from others; she was also "slow," as she put it. What we both had in common was an ability to feel—and to feel what others feel. That was the way we made our connections. We were demonstrating emotional intelligence. Knowing how to connect with others is much more valuable than knowing more than others.

As a psychologist, I use my skills to understand people's struggles. My feelings, based upon the ways they tell their stories, help me to gain perspective on their lives—and, later, insight into their stories. I don't need eyesight to see people's hearts. Mary didn't need eyesight or a high IQ to touch others when she sang. She just needed to give herself to the people in the room in order to connect. She was confirming that in life, it's not about eyesight or IQ, but about foresight and EQ.

Throughout my educational journey, I've realized that everything I've learned really doesn't count. From calculus to conversational Spanish to neuropsychology to statistics, it really doesn't matter unless I have the ability to make it significant to the world around me. That's how the teachers who found the patience, courage, and strength to teach me felt. They demonstrated this humble sentiment even as they taught me. Some special teachers knew that they were champions and experts in their areas of study, but it didn't mean anything if they couldn't connect with their students. They were extraordinary masters, amazing pros, and supernatural specialists when it came to consistently believing in the power of connection and the potential of their students. These overwhelmingly optimistic attitudes are what made me the man I am today.

People in education believed in me, and I felt it. They knew that the brain is our most powerful organ, and that education is the most powerful weapon with which to defeat life's challenges. Through their persistence, patience, and passion with me, I learned the material—but most importantly, I learned to never give up on myself. In my Spanish teacher's case, Mr. Byrdhe was a rebel and an optimist to believe that he could expect this blind student to do well. Other teachers were intimidated and unsure about what we could accomplish together. Ms. Mason was a symbol of complete strength and stubborn resiliency. Here she was, a completely blind mathematician who was teaching a completely blind student without a chalkboard or scrap paper. With precise words and Braille materials, she was able to communicate all sorts of difficult, abstract concepts to me. My life had meaning and vision because I dared to believe—and I knew that my vision for the future did not come from external vision, but from internal vision.

CHAPTER 4

Fighting in the Dark

As a blind pre-teen and early adolescent, I had few opportunities for any regular, competitive participation in sports. That was ironic, given the fact that my mother was a health and physical education teacher. Over her 40-year career, she coached many sports. Some of these included track and field, basketball, baseball, softball, soccer, gymnastics, dance, tennis, and volleyball. Not only did she coach, she also participated. My mother was a superb athlete.

I remember visiting her at Shoemaker Middle School in West Philly when I was 13 years old. "Okay, this is how you shoot a free throw!" her voice boomed through the gymnasium. "You bend your knees, push off, and with one hand behind and one hand on the side of the ball, flick your wrist!" Then I heard the sound of a basketball swishing through a basketball hoop. She had done it on her first try. She repeated the directions, and made the shot again; then repeated the directions at least three more times, and shot the basketball through the net again and again and again. She made it look easy. She bragged to friends and family about playing pickup games against some poor teenage boy who thought he was "all that" in basketball. She could play tough defense and hit shots from the outside: a humbling agent to put any kid back in their place.

Mom was no joke. Not only did she give excellent instruction and back it up with powerful play, she believed in every athlete who came to her. She never gave up on any kid, either on or off the court. In the case of kids who expressed arrogance, she had a knack for breaking them down and then building them back up again.

I was blessed to have a coach for my mother. She gave firm, clear instruction, and set high expectations when it came to my schoolwork, homework, and household chores. She also expected that I respect her and follow her directions. These were great values to instill in me, but it was also tough. That booming voice didn't just stop at the gymnasium doors when she left her job; it continued in our home. It was like hearing a drill sergeant barking out commands. She loudly and forcefully gave orders in the home, even to clean a room, redo a math problem correctly, or simply go to bed. She didn't pull any punches. She believed in me, too, and didn't believe she was being too hard on me, but felt instead that she was building my character and tolerance for frustration, pain, and adversity.

After I lost my eyesight, I was not the athletic type. I was overweight, out of shape, and emotionally vulnerable. I was not equipped mentally or physically for sports boot camp. My temperament was better suited to a relaxing trip to the beach. Once my eye problems started, medical permission to exercise was off and on, depending upon my eye condition. I was forced to stay in the house, because no one knew what a blind kid could do for fun. "Stay inside...stay on the porch...don't move..." were some of the sentiments expressed by my family.

This was understandable, because by the age of thirteen, I had had thirteen operations in a failing effort to save my eyesight. I was seen as fragile and weak, and if any more physical injuries arose, it would be a catastrophe. I'm sure my mother felt responsible for my blindness, as many parents would—because parents have the desire to protect their children from anything and everything. The truth of the matter is that we are all vulnerable, and cannot protect our children against much. In life, anything can happen, but that doesn't keep us from trying. My grandmother, who babysat me, was sure not to let me out of her sight. Every step I took was watched in fear. Everyone was scared. Everyone but me, of course.

The best thing about being a child was that I did not know all of the horrible things that could happen to me. My mother and grandmother both had very elaborate fantasy worlds. As an adult, I understand. In life, one witnesses so many horrible, scary events, and that can make a person uneasy. I didn't picture myself falling down three steps, breaking my neck, and then being confined to a wheelchair—but they did. I didn't imagine myself trying to play outside and slamming myself into a pole...but they did. And I didn't picture myself getting hit by a car; but of course, they shuddered at the thought. All I knew was that I was the same kid I had been before I lost my eyesight. If I had played tag outside before, I still wished to do so after losing my sight. If I raced, I wanted to do it after I was blind; and if I pushed the envelope regarding rules, I did the same as a blind kid.

I found all kinds of ways to push the boundaries. When I told my grandmother I was going outside to sit on the porch, somehow, some way, I found myself on the sidewalk playing tag with our neighbor Corey. He would try to walk past me as quietly as possible, and I would listen for his footsteps. When I heard a tiny muffle of a tap, I skipped to the left or right and tagged him. We had fun. He was so creative, he decided I could do the same with him, and he would close his eyes, too. Then I would try to tippy-toe past him, and he would listen for my footsteps, and tag me when he heard me go by. When my grandmother caught me, she'd get me back up on that porch, safe and secure. Other times, while restricted in the house, I would expel some excess energy. I'd drop down and do some sit-ups or push-ups, and she'd comment, "Be careful, now!" Sometimes, when I couldn't sneak my way outside, I would challenge any of the other babysat kids to a match of arm-wrestling. That sometimes turned into "tussling," as she called it. "I hear you back there. Stop all that tussling!" my grandmother would yell from the living room back to the breakfast room, where we were watching Bugs Bunny on a black-and-white television set. I found ways to have fun even when I wasn't allowed.

When I reached high school, I was only 5 feet 4 inches tall, and I packed on weight. I used to check in with my school nurse from time to time to check my weight, but it rose steadily in my ninth-grade year: 185, 195, and then as high as 207. Games of adaptive, blind tag when I was eleven, combined with an occasional push-up or sit-up, didn't keep me from packing on the pounds. Besides, in my family, if they love you, they feed you; and after I became blind, they loved me wildly! Just imagine macaroni and cheese, bread pudding, sweet potato pie, lemon cake, and many other tasty foods thrown my way. I accepted all of their love. Imagine me thankful, and praying, "Heavenly Father, thank you for this food I'm about to receive. AMEN! AMEN! AMEN!!!"

My mother not only told stories illustrating her athletic prowess, she also told great tales of triumph. They could be about some kid saying, "I can't." She would have a tough-love talk with him: "Boy, you better act like you know!" Later the same day, that kid would be breaking all sorts of records while competing. Other stories were about the passion of her students, crying their eyes out over a last-second loss. Some kids confided in her and talked about more personal issues, like being from a broken home, missing a father in jail, or feeling enraged about a mother strung out on drugs. She knew that so many of her students were beautiful, but they all had long roads behind them and ahead of them due to their individual backgrounds, talents, and challenges.

I remember one story she told me that has stayed with me for decades. It was about a little eleven-year-old girl with a "permanent smile." My mother loved teaching students with special-education accommodations. Many of these kids were intellectually disabled, physically disabled, or autistic, but that never stopped my mother from believing in them. She didn't feel sorry for kids just because they were disabled. One cool autumn morning, a class of students came to her. One of the students was a little girl with an intellectual disability. Her smile was on her face as if it had been drawn on. She had a look of ignorant bliss. She didn't talk much...just smiled. She loved gym, and couldn't wait for Ms. Watson's class.

My mother decided that day to play a team competition based upon shooting basketballs into a hoop. There would be two lines of kids. One line would compete against the other. Each child would dribble their team's basketball up to the hoop and then shoot the ball into the basket. Then, the next person in line would shoot a basket. The first team in which all members made a basket would win!

During team events, there's always an awkward moment during the choosing of the team. Kids want to play with their friends, or play with other great athletes. This little girl appeared to have limited social skills and physical talent. She was in bad shape to be picked. One little boy in her class begged that she wouldn't be on his team, so my mother allowed them both to be on opposite teams. My mother gave the instructions, blew her whistle, and the children began to play. Balls bounced wildly up to the baskets. Students threw up air balls, bricks, and missed shots, but eventually, shots were being made. Kids cheered for their teammates: "Yay! You made it! Yay! Go, go, go!" Before they knew it, it was down to the last kid against the last kid, and guess who was at the end of each line? The girl with the permanent smile—and the boy who had protested against her being on his team. I think Mom orchestrated this setup.

The two of them bounced the balls up to their respective hoops. The little girl was smiling, of course, and double-dribbled up to the hoop with two hands. The little boy tried to do it with one. They started to shoot. Her shots went straight up in the air. She jumped, and the ball went directly up: not toward the basket or anything. They didn't even touch the basket. The little boy's balls kept going around the hoop and out. His shots were getting closer and closer, but none would drop.

Then, for some reason—somehow, some way—the little girl retrieved her last missed shot, grabbed her ball, jumped straight up into the air, hurled the ball up underhanded...and it went into the basket. The class erupted. It was unbelievable. Of course, she was already smiling and jumping and clapping her hands anyway. The little boy who hadn't wanted her on his team was in disbelief. Even though my mother was surprised, she was not shocked. She never gave up on any child. She knew that anything impossible can become possible, if you believe in yourself. In sports, the underdog can win; if the underdog never did, games would never be played.

In life, so many of us have the backgrounds of "losers." Some aren't born on the "right side of the tracks," others are born into families that are neglectful and abusive, and still others have all the chips stacked against them; but that doesn't mean they are doomed to fail.

My mother's passion for sports spilled over to me. I became a Philadelphia Eagles fan, and loved to listen to their games on the radio. Even though I listened to the games, I often told classmates I loved watching them. Some seemed uncomfortable and awkward when I used the words watch and see, and they hesitated to talk to me about sports, or looked embarrassed trying. "Hey, Dre, did you, um, um, see, I mean, um, listen–to–the–game? That touchdown pass, um, sounded–nice...didn't it?" I usually would reply, "Yeah, man, I saw the game, the Eagles looked real good!"

I have always been fascinated with the amount of detail and accuracy possessed by radio sports announcers. I sat with anticipation next to my radio, imagined football plays, and even recorded games on a cassette tape to later make more recordings of exciting plays over exciting music. I would spend every Sunday talking to my buddies— Dana, Carnell, Rodney, or Jonathan—while the football games were on, and they would explain their own reactions. I fantasized about the days I had pretended to play football at recess at Commodore John Barry Elementary School, weaving and bobbing past defenders. I thought about how I had actually thrown a football at the age of eight to Gordon, a neighborhood friend of my cousin Rodney. We played a quick game, and I said I would be the quarterback. Gordon went out for the pass, and Rodney covered him. My small hands could barely hold the kid-sized football. I cocked my arm back and threw. It was actually a spiral, and made it into Gordon's hands. He ran past the third pole...and that was a touchdown.

I had a passion for sports, but after I lost my eyesight and put on weight, I thought, "What now?"

Would I ever play sports? Would I ever experience the thrill of victory and the agony of defeat? Would I ever get the chance to bond with teammates and share in masculine camaraderie again?

My mother told me that blind kids actually joined wrestling teams and won; but even though she had informed me of the options, she still was scared. She was scared of her child getting hurt, getting taken advantage of, and failing. In spite of her feelings of trepidation and fear, she decided to give me the green light to join the wrestling team. She gave me permission to wrestle blind, compete, battle against my peers, and fight in the dark. From the moment my mother believed in me and gave me permission, my life has never been the same.

The day I decided to join the wrestling team, I approached Coach Flaxman. I did not know him beforehand, so when I approached him, I didn't know what to expect. He usually finished teaching a fifth-period biology course in the same classroom where I had chemistry during sixth period. As the classes were changing, I knew I could go up to him. "Um, Mr. Flaxman? I'm wondering if I could try out for the wrestling team."

He paused. "Oh, really?"

"I heard that kids who are blind wrestle," I continued.

"Well, let me tell you a story," Mr. Flaxman began. "One year at a former school, we wrestled the Overbrook School for the Blind. We went in there thinking we were going to beat up on these poor blind kids. Well, when we walked out," Mr. Flaxman began to chuckle, "One of my guys had a neck brace on, another was on crutches, and another had his arm in a sling. You want to come out for the wrestling team? Sure!"

I was delighted, but also scared, because I didn't know what to expect. One of my friends, Jonathan White, was in my sixth-grade chemistry class, and I told him I was going to try wrestling. He was elated for me, and even said that since football season was over, he needed some other sport to try, and was thinking about wrestling.

The first month of practices were designed to get athletes in shape, and all took place outside. The wrestling captains led these practices. The workout consisted of lots of counting and yelling in unison, rapidly changing stretches and calisthenics, and finally, a one-and-a-half-mile run. Remember, I was from a family who loved me and fed me, and I had had absolutely no exercise for over five years. Needless to say, I couldn't do anything. One push-up, one sit-up, or one jumping jack was too much for me. I had a headache immediately. For that first month of trying to join in with the exercises, I was in so much pain. I was out of breath instantly, my body cramped up easily, and my head throbbed. I was also with a bunch of guys who had never known a blind wrestler, so they were constantly trying to explain to me how to do a particular exercise or stretch. Sometimes, the teachings started off with verbal directions; then I would feel another athlete's body in a pose; and then I'd try. Sometimes, I never really got what they were trying to get me to do, and they would say, "Um, you got the general idea." I felt like quitting every day. I never finished the run or any of the other exercises. I was tight and inflexible. I weighed in at heavyweight, and that was tough. I was 5 feet 5 inches tall, and weighed 207 pounds. I'm so glad I didn't quit.

When real practices started in November, we met up on the wrestling mat. Jonathan and I joined, and were in the beginners' group. We had to learn the basics of standing, takedowns, how to control the opponent on the mat, and how to defend yourself against being pinned. All of the teaching I received was from someone doing the moves on me first—that's how I got a picture in my mind of how the move should feel. I remember Coach Flaxman demonstrating a single-leg takedown on me. I was standing up, and he grabbed my leg and swung me around in a circle. I went flying into the mat. Wow, he was strong. We learned that the best way to teach me was for me to experience the move. If I had the move done to me, I could then do it to others. I was learning by feel. Of course, my brain had to process all of the intricate movements and subtleties, but the real understanding of the move came from doing it. In life, we learn by doing. We can read lots of books and pontificate about how things should be done, but if you don't truly experience life and hardship, you will never really know.

For the last three years of high school, I wrestled. It started with junior varsity, and by my junior year, I was wrestling varsity. My first year, I was happy just to wrestle JV; but when our varsity heavyweight unexpectedly left our team, I was given the spot.

Our varsity heavyweight had been a 17-year-old boy named Michael Manley. He was quite manly: strong, quick, and smart. He actually wrestled just one year—his senior year. During that year, he wrestled varsity. He was also my primary practice partner. Wow, he was tough. I remember that he did not baby me, but instead pushed me to be my best. I remember that he was one of my first cheerleaders.

Even though we were learning moves at the same time, he seemed to be able to learn them from Coach Flaxman immediately, then execute them with power and determination. I, on the other hand, was flabby, often became winded, and needed lots of practice.

I remember Mike's first regular-season match. It was intense. I heard everyone screaming and yelling during his match. At one point, people were yelling, "Yeah, yeah, yeah!" and then they were saying "No, no, no! Get up!" By the time someone told me what was happening, his match had changed direction quickly. When we thought he was pinned, he didn't give up. My teammate standing next to me said, "Bridge! Get off your back!" I heard the referee's whistle, and a hand-slap to the mat done with finality and certainty. Not being able to see what happened, I wasn't sure if Mike had lost. The cheers from the other team's players had come to a hush as my teammates were cheering and going crazy. Mike had won. It was explained to me that he had bridged while his opponent was pinning him, twisted, reversed his opponent's position, and landed on top for a Central victory.

My first match, on the other hand, was anti-climactic. I was nervous, and barely fit into my singlet. If you've seen those wrestling singlets, you will understand what I'm saying. They are an insecure teenage boy's worst enemy. I was embarrassed; now all of my teenage fat could show, and be seen by everyone. I doubted myself. Of course, the heavyweight JV match was the last of the day. I had to endure the wait, and what made it so difficult was hearing everyone say, "Wow, look at that huge guy on the other side!" I kept hearing this while waiting for my match—and throughout the entire competition.

My opponent was huge. We started off our match like two awkward-looking dancers. Neither of us knew what to do. Our arms extended and wrapped around each other's shoulders. I felt his blubbery body bounce against mine, then his body weight shifted to trip me. His leg stuck out beyond his massive belly, and behind my jiggly leg. I was so nervous; I didn't react to stop it. Then, I fell—flat on my back. Oops, that hurt. That was the wrong thing to do, I thought to myself. Then, with all of his weight, my opponent flopped on my body with a massive boom! He continued to punish my joints, arteries, and ligaments as he mashed my body, crawling from my legs to my chest. I was crushed. He didn't know what to do to get me completely on my back, so I guess his natural impulse was to use all 275 pounds of himself to flop up and down, smothering me into the mat. I felt I was surely about to die. It's amazing when you're in situations like these—you have a dozen thoughts in one moment. Why am I doing this? How did I get into this situation? What the heck is going on? And at that point, I heard a voice in my left ear. "Get up, babe! Get up! High leg over!" It was Mike's voice. He was just a few feet away from me. I wish I could have tagged him in, and that he could have "creamed that dude," but I couldn't.

When I heard his voice, I felt a rush of energy. I started to bridge, and my neck had never been tested more severely than it was in that moment. I tried with everything I had to get out of that pin hold. Mike said it again, "That's it! You almost are

out!" I squirmed and tried to bridge my body up using my neck and legs as a support to keep my
shoulders from touching the mat. I couldn't hold
myself and my gargantuan opponent anymore. My
body failed me, and stopped thrusting. Then I heard
the quiet of the gym, the whistle, and the referee's
hand-slap the mat. It was over...thank God for me.
My neck was about to snap. It had been used like a
car jack: pushing up over 400 pounds to keep my
back from touching the mat for 10 or 15 seconds,
which had seemed like an eternity. Thank God I still
have the use of my hands and legs after that event. I
am so thankful to Mike, for that moment and for so
many others over the course of that wrestling year.
He was an excellent practice partner, a role model
to me, a guide, and a friend. Most importantly, when
I was literally down and flat on my back, he believed
in me, and I will never forget that.

Much of our team's camaraderie and togeth-
erness came from our coach. He was serious about
wrestling, but he also knew the importance of relationship and fun. Coach Flaxman was great, and often teased his wrestlers. He laughed so much. He
made fun of us, called all of us "ugly," and said, "If
you think you're in pain, how do you think I feel
looking at you?" And when we couldn't get a move
or became silly in practice, he accused us of taking
"dumb pills." He didn't discriminate, either. He
made fun of me, too, and playfully made us all laugh
at ourselves. For teenage boys, that is so important.

As a teenager, you are so concerned about how you look, how others see you, and if you fit in. Coach made sure we could laugh at ourselves.

After another month of learning moves by touch and keeping a light attitude, I started to actually get used to the workouts. The headaches passed, and I started to progress. I could do 10 push-ups, then 20 push-ups. I could do 25 sit-ups with confidence, and without struggle. I was starting to learn moves by sensing the feel of my opponent's body. When I felt their level shift up or down, I knew they were getting ready to go for a move. When I felt their shoulders twist, they were turning and trying to do something else; and when I felt them come in close, they were trying to control my body movements, as well.

I remember my first win as a JV wrestler. I kept practicing the same move over and over in my head. I was going to start with the obligatory touch-start, my hands clasped with my opponent's hands. The ref would say "Wrestle!" and I would grab his wrist and yank him toward me, then grab his leg. When the match came, I did it, and it happened to perfection. It wasn't so much that I was all that great, but that we both were all that bad. I fell on top of this poor kid, who was as pudgy as me, and then I just tried to hold him down somehow. Now I was the gargantuan, massive opponent squishing some poor kid. We both rolled around. He was on top of me, then I was on top of him, and at the end of the match, I was pinning him. Instead of him bridging up and down on his poor neck, he just kept rolling from one shoulder to the other. I wished that I had known that move, but I'm sure he made that up on the spot to give himself his own slow death. The ref's hand slapped the mat, and he blew the whistle. I had won! I could not believe it. Everyone mobbed me. It felt like thousands of hands touching me all over, patting me on my back, rubbing my head, and hugging me. One of my teammates asked me, "How does it feel, winning your first match!?" I responded, "I'm going to Disney World!" We all laughed. What a great feeling to win, to be cheered for, and for people to believe in me.

Over the three years I wrestled in high school, I transformed. I went from a round mound to a strong, confident, 5 foot 10 inch, 167-pound machine. After my initial days of aches and pains, I learned to embrace muscle soreness as character-building medicine. I got slammed on my face and dragged across the mat, and was often exhausted after my hour-and-a-half commute home. My days were long in high school, as I got up at 5:15 a.m. and didn't get home until 7:00 p.m.; and still, I had to complete my homework. I even managed to have a social life, too.

Wrestling did not subtract from my time, but, in fact, added to it. I became more popular. The school knew that there was a blind kid who wrestled, and that he was actually good. After taking over on varsity at the end of my sophomore year, I was 5 and 1 my junior year, and 14 and 2 my senior year. I was a force to be reckoned with. After I slowly lost the weight, my competitors also shrank in body size. At one point, I had to wrestle guys as big as 275 pounds; but after dropping two weight classes, I was wrestling other boys who felt like feathers to me. I took advice from my coach to work hard during the off-season on my strength and conditioning. My mother took me to the track during the summer, and let me run around it. I was initially unsure of how to run around the track safely, and at my own pace. We tried to get my eight-year-old sister Le'Nell to run with me. She was so cute and enthusiastic, and so happy to spend time with her mom and brother; but she could not keep up with me in order to tell me which way to go and warn me of the turns and bends in the track. Early on, we realized this fact when we were running, and I left her behind. When the first curve came up, I intuitively had the feeling to fade left, and then a little more left again; and then I was on the next straightaway. "I'm doing it!" I thought to myself. That, unfortunately, was premature, because at the next curve, I made a misjudgment, and kept going straight when my turn came up. I ended up running off the track and sliding into a ditch. All I heard was, "Where did he go?"

"I don't know!"

When I got myself to my knees and started to climb out of that ditch, my mother said it looked like a hand coming out of the ground—like a scene from *Night of The Living Dead*. We laugh about that moment still. Even after my near-death experience, I thought to myself, how can I make this work? I can't just quit and say, "Oh, well, there's no way to do this. I cannot run. I just won't be as prepared as everyone else. I will just have to give up on being good." Instead, I decided to take my cane and drag it alongside of me. In this way, I was able to follow a small ridge that ran around the inner side of the track. Before I knew it, I was running with speed and determination: four times around, five times around, eight times around, ten times around. The sweat dripped from my body in the hot, humid August air. Believe it or not, it felt great! I was not only running and breathing heavily, but I was living. I started to discover that through running, I felt free. My body could feel the endorphins from pumping, extending, and retracting. I was able to feel!

I did not approach this situation as most people would expect. "You're blind, don't try. It's too dangerous. What if you ran down that ditch again? What if you ran into someone? What if you got hurt? And even after that, would it be worth it?" Instead, I allowed myself to dream as I ran around that track. I pictured myself pinning opponents, I felt my arm being raised by the referee in victory, and I heard my coach and teammates say, "Go!" Not only did I rediscover running, but I also discovered muscle memory and strength. I did push-ups and sit-ups like crazy at home during the summer times and off-season. I started off with 10, then 20, and then I reached 50. Soon I was doing 75, then 100 push-ups at night. Before I knew it, I was doing 500 push-ups before bed in sets of 80. I did hundreds of sit-ups, as well. I started to feel my arms and body, and noticed that it was changing. I also discovered a dip bar. The days of being teased for being overweight and needing a bra were over. My coach and teammates complimented me on the changes they were noticing, and there were actually some girls who noticed, too. "Andre, you work out?" Wow, I was feeling like a young man.

With my increase in ability came an increase in responsibility. I did not have easy matches. The word got around that there was a blind wrestler at Central, and that he was pretty good. It got around so much that The Daily News came to interview me. The headline was "I'm Blessed!" –and that was exactly what I felt about my blindness and the opportunity to wrestle. It had changed me. It showed me that just because I had a disability, that didn't mean that I could give up on myself, or that others should give up on me. "When life gives you lemons, you make lemonade."

My mother embodied this sentiment. She believed in willing things to happen in life, and would become enraged if I ever said I could not do something. She literally poured determination into me.

No matter what it was about, she never accepted quitting.

I remember one really tough match at the beginning of my senior year. People had started to find out that my favorite move was the Peterson Roll, and they were defending against it. The roll is sort of like throwing someone over your shoulder, but you're both on your hands and knees. For a moment, your opponent feels in control of you; and then suddenly, you toss him over your shoulder, he flops on the mat in front of you, and you pin him for the win. I had great success with the move. It often lured my opponents into thinking they had me down, and then I would trick them. It was almost like my blindness gave them a sense of false confidence and false security: "I got him now!" People started to learn that this blind guy was good. The message was: Don't let your guard down and lose just because you're underestimating him.

Once other teams knew about "the roll," they were coaching against that move. Without it, I had to do something else. Well, in this particular match, I could not roll my opponent off of my back. He had my arms wrapped up, and my head on the mat. Wow, he's strong, I thought to myself. This was one of those matches during which I thought to myself, this is not going to be pretty. Hopefully, something will happen. The irony was that nothing was going to happen until I made it happen—and I wasn't making anything happen. He had me bottled up and contained. I felt weak. Then, from the sidelines, my coach, my teammates, and everyone around me started yelling, "Andre, get up!" They were yelling out moves, techniques, and strategies. "Step up! Pull your arm out! Wrist control!" I couldn't do anything. Then, over everyone else's voices, I heard a familiar one: "Andre, get up. Now!" It was my mother's voice, and I did what any obedient child would have done. I did what she said, and stood up. My legs drove upward, and my arms pushed up. I grabbed his wrist, switched my hips, drove him to the mat, and pinned him for the win. Everyone asked, "What happened, all of a sudden? You got a surge of energy?" Even the referee said after the match that I had had a surge of strength.

It is obvious to me that my mother's voice was the most important for me to hear in that moment. Sometimes, while wrestling, there would be so many people yelling and screaming, but only certain voices that I needed to listen to. In most situations, I listened for my coach; but in that situation, when I was doubting myself and didn't know if I could do it, my mother's voice was the most crucial.

In life, I have realized that many voices yell and scream at us. People tell us what to do: "Go left! Go right! That's the wrong decision! No!" There is usually one important voice you must hear over all others. Sometimes, it's your mother's; sometimes, it's your father's; and sometimes, it's your own. As I've grown older, as an adult, I've felt it to be God's.

That voice is pulling me out of the despair of defeat, pulling me out of a hole, giving me wisdom and guidance. Sometimes, that voice is a clear, soothing, confident whisper. God uses all sorts of situations and people to speak to us when times get tough. Wrestling taught me that when times get tough, that's not the time to quit. In fact, that's when it's time to get strong.

Wrestling also taught me a great deal academically, socially, and athletically. First, in order to improve athletically, fatigue was part of the natural process; and if I didn't get tired, I wouldn't get strong. In life, too, if you don't get tired, you won't get strong. Muscles have to be broken down and built back up again. This scheme works not just for the body, but also for the mind and heart. Failures, setbacks, and heartbreaks all teach us how to persevere. When you are absolutely exhausted and pushed to the point of quitting, you cannot; and for those who are never pushed to that point, they are easy to push flat on their backs to get pinned.

My time wrestling for Central was the best time of my life. I was "one of the guys," all because my mother, my coaches, and my teammates had given me a chance. Instead of looking at me as just some overweight blind kid who was fantasizing, they helped my dreams to come true. They cheered for me, yelled in my face when they knew I was being lazy or "dogging it," and helped me pick myself up when times were tough. I could never have repaid all of my coaches and teammates for what they gave me: a sense of belonging, a sense of positive self-esteem, a sense of personal power. What's amazing is that they could not have given me a strong sense of self unless they actually challenged me, pushed me, and made me feel pain. It made me resilient. Not only was I resilient, but I became a good wrestler. I won most of my matches without sight, but with the courage to see a vision while still living in the dark.

Dontae Wilson, Adam Truax, Alex Zuchman, Alex Cohen, Beji, Sal, Mike Manley, Mike Thumbel, Ernest, Tao, Eltor, Dashaun, Ryan, Billy, Scott, Colin, and so many others took me seriously. I remember the day I accepted the Sportsman of the Year award from the Philadelphia School District for wrestling, which was presented to me at a dinner. I was brought to the podium by our captain, Sal Bianco, and I was speechless. I didn't know what to say when they placed a big plaque in my hands with the words "Sportsman of the Year to Andre Watson" embossed in Braille. It was amazing. Lots of speeches were given to thank people. They did not ask me to speak, but I would have thanked every competitor in that room who had once tried to rip my head off. And most people would ask, "Why?" It's because I was legitimized and validated as a growing man. I was taken seriously, and seen as being just as good as anyone else. I've strived in so many arenas since that moment just to "get on the mat" of life in order to take on new challenges and experience new thrills.

At the end of my senior year of wrestling, I managed to become third team/all public and Sportsman of the Year for the Philadelphia Public League. It means so much to me still that my hard work and growth were recognized. The thing I was so thankful for was not so much having the opportunity to compete or even the opportunity to win, but the opportunity to lose. It meant so much to me that others gave me the chance to compete against them in order to beat me. In that context, I was like everyone else. I was experiencing the agony of defeat and the thrill of victory. I was taken seriously as an athlete, and most of all, I became feared for my strengths, determination, and undying spirit.

After high school wrestling, I joined the wrestling team at the University of Pittsburgh. If high school wrestling had been tough, college wrestling was tough times ten. I had loved the camaraderie of high school wrestling, and wanted to experience that once again. When I joined, I was just a walk-on, and was not drafted. My coach was also very doubtful about me joining. He kept asking me, "Are you sure? You really want to do this?" I didn't flinch, and said I did. I lasted the entire year, and didn't miss a workout or a practice. I was there every day, twice a day, and worked my butt off. I didn't receive much coaching while wrestling in college. Everyone else on the team had been competing since they were kids, and there I was, a blind guy who had only been wrestling for a few years. I ended up becoming a powerful wrestler, just a step behind the starter. I gave each of my teammates a competitive challenge, and even worked my way into a second-string position. I ended up winning a national championship for blind wrestling, and dominated the blind wrestlers that year.

Afterwards, I became disillusioned with the atmosphere of a college team versus a high school team. It was run very much like a business, and things like team camaraderie came second to individual performance. Those who were getting wrestling scholarships had all of the pressure on them to win. That made me even more determined to outwork everyone else on the team.

My best compliment came during a meeting in the locker room. Our assistant coach, Coach Payne, had gotten everyone's attention, and was looking at a sheet of paper. "Guys, what's up? You guys are missing your morning workouts. The only one who has not missed a morning weightlifting session is Andre. He has just as much as you guys to do, and he gets it done." By the end of the wrestling season, the head coach kept asking me, "Are you sure you don't want to come back next year? You can give us plenty." I knew that if I gave college wrestling four years of my life, I would have been good, but other sports and pursuits were in the stars for me.

For the next 15 years after college wrestling, I took on four different sports. I obtained my "pre-black belt" in Tang Soo Do, a black belt in Judo, and two years of experience with Brazilian Jujitsu. I also won three national championships in goalball, a sport for blind athletes, and played on the U.S. national team.

After high school wrestling ended, and after I had become totally exhausted and disillusioned as a result of college wrestling, I thought that my days of fighting in the dark were over. Thankfully, I was wrong. While in college, I met a blind, buff dude named Bob Lichtenfels. I remember the first time I met Bob in the Disability Students' Office at the University of Pittsburgh. I was there making arrangements for some book of mine to be scanned into an electronic format, and he walked in. He tapped into the office with his cane, chuckled, and said "Hi!" to everyone. When asked by one of the volunteers how he was doing, he said, "Just fine. Just jumped over that bar that runs along Fifth Avenue to avoid getting hit by a bus." What?! I thought to myself. What kind of daredevil is this? I later got to meet Bob, and he became a great role model for me.

Bob was a few years older, and had lots of life lessons to share as a blind man and athlete. He embodied hard work, guts, and determination. Previous to my arrival at Pitt, he had joined the wrestling team, as well. He was really strong, and understood the sport inside and out. His dreams came to an end after he and his girlfriend (now his wife) were in a car accident. It turned out that a friend of his was driving Bob and Sue somewhere, lost control, and slammed into a tree. Bob told me that Sue was paralyzed from that accident. Prior to the accident, she had been blind; and now, she was blind and in a wheelchair. She had also been a great athlete, and loved sports for the blind. Today, she is the founder of SportsVision, a nonprofit organization for the blind in Pennsylvania.

Bob and Sue had a compelling story, and I thought they were extraordinary people—not just because they were blind, but because they were blind and like everyone else. In them, I saw a future for myself. They had degrees and friends, and were incredibly active.

Bob had encouraged me to join the wrestling team at Pitt. He saw potential in my athleticism, and thought I had a lot to offer. He also invited me to play goalball—the only sport in the world designed for blind athletes. Goalball is a three-on-three sport in which all players defend a net as if they are goalies, by sliding on the floor to block a ball with bells in it. When a player blocks the ball, he stands up and rolls it as fast as he can to toward the opposite net. There, players block the ball.

This sport was rugged. The ball could come so fast at your head; it could literally knock you out if you didn't block your face. Players had to get suited up in all kinds of hip pads, elbow pads, kneepads, and, of course, jock straps and cups for protection. All players wore sleep shades or masks that blocked their vision, so that no one could see the ball. Even though the players were blind, some actually had a good bit of usable vision. In goalball, all of us were equal. What is most interesting is watching someone who is sighted play goalball for the first time. It can be terrifying. You don't know where the ball is, and you feel disoriented. The most frightening thing is that you are in the dark.

While playing goalball for ten years, I joined up with players in Philadelphia: John Mulhern and Greg Gontaryk. We ended up dominating U.S. goalball in the early 2000s, and won three championships and countless national tournaments. We also went to Canada, and beat their best players several times.

Goalball gave me a real sense of pride as a blind person. There I was, playing a sport with blind people, sharing ideas about life, and being encouraged. Some of the players were professionals: counselors, teachers, professors, lawyers, and lifetime athletes. Others were college students, husbands, wives, and parents. Goalball gave me something I had never experienced while growing up. I was part of a community of people like me—and in that environment, I could be myself. I grew and flourished.

While playing goalball, I moved back to Philadelphia for graduate school at Widener University. At Widener, I continued playing goalball. While Greg, John, and I were on a tear to dominate U.S. goalball, we were also cross-training with teacher Gwen Smith. Gwen was a neighbor of Greg's, and she approached him about starting a Tang Soo Do class for blind athletes. Greg invited John, myself, Darren Daily, John's brother Steve, and a bunch of other blind goalball athletes.

Gwen didn't take it easy on us at all. She and her assistants, Tom and Mike, used to work us to death. Some of the most difficult workouts included her telling us to start doing jumping jacks, and then disappearing to answer a ringing phone in the office of the dojo. We had no idea when she would return. I think one time we counted up to 500 while doing those jumping jacks. She made us do push-ups on our knuckles, stood on our legs while we were in a butterfly stretch to make our knees touch the floor, and had us break boards with our hands. I remember once, while testing for a belt, her sensei handed Greg and me a board and said, "Break this board." We were both dumbfounded, and didn't know how we should do it. In the heat of the moment, I held the board in my left hand, and chopped straight down to break it. It worked, and I was shocked I could do such a thing.

We also sparred. We put on headgear, boxing gloves, and bells. The bells helped us know where we were. We learned how to use the staff and defend against punches and grabs, and during one class, another instructor even taught us how to defend ourselves against someone pointing a gun at us. Gwen was an awesome teacher. She was a black woman of about fifty: short and thick, but muscular and hard where she needed to be. When she kicked us, we flew back, and when she threw punches at us, we flinched at the wind across our faces.

During the six years I did Tang Soo Do, I became stronger, faster, harder, and more focused in goalball and my athleticism. I learned how to do every jumping, spinning, and jumping/spinning kick. I was pushed to a new type of physical flexibility, and I found another place to believe in myself.

Gwen believed in her students. At some schools, teachers would shy away from having a blind student; but she welcomed us, and wanted to have us. See, Gwen had two adult daughters, one of whom was slightly older than me. She was a martial artist, as well, and incredibly talented. Gwen's other adult daughter was severely disabled, blind, and wheelchair-bound. She was unable to talk, and whenever Gwen had to bring her to practices, she usually sat at the back of the room, playfully screeching or uttering the babbling sounds of a baby. At the end of class, I would hear Gwen walk over to her and say, "Hey, Sweetie," and give her one of those juicy, squeaky kisses.

Gwen's love for her class and for karate came out of her love for her children. She reinforced lessons surrounding relationships, believing in oneself, and believing in others. She taught us about integrity, concentration, perseverance, respect, obedience, self-control, humility, and having an indomitable spirit. After karate with Gwen, I felt powerful! Unfortunately, just before I was to receive my black belt in Tang Soo Do, we went through a series of changes. The school closed down, and Gwen tried to keep our visually impaired class practicing in the basement of a church. I watched our school decline from a thriving business to a class of two: just Darren and myself. Many days, it was just me. Gwen hurt her foot and had to retire, and Mike was left to teach the class. I then discontinued my time with Tang Soo Do to venture on to my most challenging athletic pursuit: Judo.

After having been away from competitive wrestling for about a decade, I was introduced to the sport of Judo. Judo was made for blind fighters. It is a sport that relies upon a keen sense of touch and awareness of your own body in space, as well as your opponent's. While competing in Judo, I met so many wonderful competitors and coaches. Dr. Mark Vink was my first coach. If my wrestling coach thought I could be great, Sensei Vink thought I could be out of this world—and that's what he trained me to do. I started learning Judo just as I had done with wrestling: by paying attention to my partner's movements, then imitating them. I traveled around the country, and even the world, with the U.S. Paralympic Judo team. I had so much support from so many people who made me tough and tenacious: Paul Latimer, Rodney Rappe, Liberty Bell Judo, and everyone at Pottstown Judo. I ended up winning countless tournaments, and won many medals for my weight class and age group among sighted fighters. While working out with the U.S. Paralympic team, I got to train with gold medalist Scott Moore, and learned what it meant to sacrifice everything you have to achieve a goal.

In 2008, I worked so hard, and went to China for the Paralympics. What a once-in-a-lifetime experience! I had the opportunity to compete against the best athletes in the world. Whenever I competed internationally against other blind fighters, I found that they were better than many of the sighted competitors I had faced at home. I think that's because these fighters had gone through some of the same experiences I'd had. They were denied so many things in life, but through Judo, they were allowed to excel, compete, and feel powerful! These blind athletes have so much to teach the world. And I'm not just saying this in a warm and fuzzy way. These athletes were the best—not only among blind fighters, but among all fighters. Through Judo, I was able to observe how blind people could not only excel, but be better than most in any field. I have countless stories of fighting, winning, screaming, yelling, crying, and being victorious, because so many people believed in me.

After Judo, I started the Audio Dart Club of Delaware Valley. If Judo wasn't daring enough, darts for the blind certainly would be. In Audio Darts, all players wear a blindfold, and shoot at a standard board eight feet away. Through Audio Darts, I met so many wonderful people across the country. Darts for the blind is amazing in so many ways. First, the thought of blind people throwing darts is incredibly scary. People cannot imagine. If I really want a good laugh, I talk about darts with friends while on public transportation, and just wait for other passengers to chime in. "What?! Blind people play darts? Does anyone ever get hurt? Do they actually hit the board?" All of these are questions and comments I regularly hear. I usually reply that we only get hit when we throw the darts at each other on purpose. If you're wondering if we hit the dartboard, we do very well. I've watched players hit bull's-eyes when they needed to win. At other times, I've witnessed players hit exceedingly small spaces on the board in order to get a particular point count.

Audio Darts is incredibly difficult in the be-ginning. I consider it a character-building tool, es-pecially for those who rely upon their sight. It takes lots of patience, resilience, and practice to just hit the board when blindfolded. Many people cannot take the frustration of missing over and over again. When I played Audio Darts for the first time, I remember hitting my basement wall over and over again, and wondering if I would ever get this game. Well, I ended up winning a number of individual and team competitions around the country among blind players; and if you think that's great, imagine the look on my sighted friends' and family's faces when I beat them. One friend said, "I can see. You are blind. We play darts. I throw the dart, I miss. You are blind and throw the dart, and you hit a bull's-eye. Something's wrong here." It is a pleasure teaching blind people darts, because it shows sighted and blind people alike that just because you're in the dark doesn't mean you can't hit the mark—both literally and figuratively. It is a game that many people think is solely dependent upon sight...but as Allen Iverson would say, "Practice."

The most important part of sports is winning, right? I absolutely loved every game, match, and competition I ever competed in. I would not be the man I am today without sports. I am convinced 100 times over that for minorities, the disabled, women, or anyone else who is marginalized, playing sports does a ton of good for self-esteem. More importantly, it is the relationships with people that make the difference. I often wonder what happened to some of the friends I played so many sports with, especially wrestling. I have been able to reconnect with some of my old teammates over 20 years later.

I am still friends with Adam Truax from my high school wrestling team. Adam was the captain during our senior year. In recent years, we visited our high school wrestling coach, Coach Flaxman, at his home. We laughed and reminisced about the good times and the relationships we shared. Adam and I have visited the coach a few times since high school, and it has always been great. On one drive back from Coach's home, Adam was dropping me off after a time of gut-busting reminiscing. We had spent a few hours reliving our battles on the wrestling mat, and how we had screeched and screamed for each other. He said to me, "Man, wrestling made such a difference in my life. I thank Coach so much for what he did for me," and I agreed. Out of nowhere, he said, "Love you, man," and I told him that I loved him, too, and we hugged. We had a bromance moment, because wrestling made it so. We were able to bond over one common goal: "Just don't get pinned!" Everyone on the team felt one big ball of emotion together—everything from fear to excitement, elation, humiliation, and most importantly, love for the sport. Sports gave us all a deeper way of seeing each other. We saw one another as more than just what we looked like, or what color we were, or how big or small we were. We saw each other's hearts and souls.

When I went to my high school reunion a few years ago, ready to get caught up with all of my old schoolmates, another really extraordinary thing happened. A woman came up to me and said, "Excuse me—did you ever know Alex Cohen in high school?" I thought, what a weird thing to ask, and replied, "Sure! Where is he?" She replied, "Right here!" And for a split second, I wondered to myself why Alex couldn't just say hello to me. He and I had wrestled together, and we graduated from high school the same year. He then bellowed out, "Dude! It's me! I'm part of the club, too!" and tapped me with his cane. I was shocked; he was blind. The two of us talked all night long. He told me how he had lost his eyesight after college, and thought about me, triumphs as a blind athlete, and our battles on the wrestling mat. He now holds a Ph.D. in marketing.

Over the years, I reconnected with others, but often wondered what had happened to my first partner, Mike Manley. He was the guy who was strong and threw me around the mat, but still believed in me when I was nothing close to an athlete. He believed in me. Whatever had happened to him? Did he go on to college? Did he continue sports somewhere else? Did he have a family? When I did a search on the Internet, I found the startling and shocking news that Manley had been sentenced to death on February 3, 2006. What? The guy who had been such a wonderful teammate was sentenced to death row for murder? I was flabbergasted. The guy I had been so thankful for, for turning me into a warrior, was now locked up behind bars. Didn't they know what kind of guy he was? Did he do it? Based upon several pages I read online, he was made out to be cold, heartless, and a killer. This was not the man I knew. His life was not the life of a criminal, and most certainly, none of his actions had been those of a criminal.

So often, we look at the news and hear about some "criminal," drug addict, or convicted felon, and instantly, we think of a monster. Michael Manley was now a monster. He was now behind steel bars, caged like an animal to punish him until he would finally be led to a room where he would be given a needle to slow his heart down and kill him. How could this be? So many times, we see criminals as "good for nothing," irredeemable, and unforgivable. When I found out that Mike was on death row in the State of Delaware, I hesitated for several years before I wrote to him. What should I say? What could I do? All I knew was that what he had done for me would never be seen or recognized by anyone. Now, he would only be known for a crime.

After a long time, I finally wrote a letter to him. I replayed our time together as teammates: how he had been there for my first fight in the dark, and how he had been a key person in my development. I went on to tell him, "You were an excellent practice partner, a role model to me, a guide, and a friend. Most importantly, when I was on my back, you believed in me, and I will never forget that. If you hadn't been in my life, my life would never have turned out to be what it is today." I know that to be true. Mike was part of a small minority who knew I could do it. I went on to tell him, "The Mike I knew was a talented, brilliant, funny, motivational, cool dude who had my back when I needed it—who propelled me to soar in my life. This guy I am reading about is not you."

After about a month, Mike wrote back. He said, "There are moments when you can doubt the person you were and believe you are at your core. So at least that young man you wrote about was real. I'm grateful you regard me in such a way. I do believe you give me too much credit. I recall that match clearly, and it's true, I did believe in you, and was proud of you, and you never quit. I'm not surprised you have achieved all that you have. You earned it, just as you earned the respect from the team, myself included." He then went on to say, "Andre, people say you have different things— courage, determination, grit—I call it heart." He then concluded, "I am thankful that our time together was beneficial. I want to thank you for the letter. Indeed, it feels at times as if I'm on the mat with you. There's a lot of weight on my chest. I just need to bridge a little longer. It sure was nice of you to yell encouragement from the sidelines...sorry it took so long to respond. It took a couple of days to get my emotions in control...I was moved."

There are so many lessons I have learned after reconnecting with my old wrestling teammates from high school. I've learned about sportsmanship, hard work, and teamwork. I've learned that if you want something, you have to be willing to sacrifice to get it. I've learned that sports help people grow in character, and get close to others. I've learned that a far-off distant memory of a high school junior varsity match can propel someone to victory. Most of all, I've learned that while fighting in the dark, you can see what people are made of—and, as Mike put it, see their "core." This is my story, the story of a blind kid who was not given a chance at much...but somebody believed in me. Ironically, it's sometimes the people you would least expect. Here I am singing the praises of a convicted murderer as a pivotal person in my life. Someone might look at him now and see him as useless, a waste of a life, a criminal, a nothing...but to me, he was everything.

My mother believed in children who were considered "slow" and "incapable" as able to accomplish the unthinkable. In sports, games are played because even though someone might be a favorite, or "look" as if they will win, sometimes, the unbelievable happens. My martial arts teachers saw possibility in me, and saw the probability of success. For this, they did not use their physical eyes, but their emotional and mental ones. In life, it's about seeing what can be. It's about imagining yourself wrestling with the trials of life, and visualizing yourself coming out on top. It's about fighting when you don't know if you are winning or losing—you just know not to give up.

CHAPTER 5

Loving in the Dark

"There's somebody for everybody—" at least that's what they say. I wasn't too sure of that claim for a long time. Years of dating in the dark had been filled with dreary, cloudy, rainy days. It all started when I was a teenager, and I wished to be liked by some girl. We often tell kids to "stay kids" and hold off on dating, but so much of what we do for children suggests romance. There are proms, dances, weddings, and all sorts of events that stir up feelings of wanting to be close to someone, intimate and treasured. The music we listen to and the shows on television encourage us to look for love and to find that "right someone," or even that "for-right-now" someone. Throughout my childhood and adolescent years, I had all sorts of infatuations.

In the third grade, there was a young girl named Lataya. I remember her pretty barrettes holding her brown hair in place as she jumped rope and ran around the schoolyard. I hardly ever spoke to her, but that didn't stop me from liking her. She was pretty, and seemed nice. She rarely got into trouble, and always seemed to have a smile on her face. I remember one time I saw her running around the playground with some boy I didn't know. I was filled with envy. We should have been running after each other, playing tag, and enjoying each other. I disliked this particular kid instantly. A few days later, on my way to school, I saw him. I ended up picking a fight with this guy by pushing him—and then I was taught a lesson. He calmly and graciously kicked my little butt. He must have been one of those fighting prodigies you hear about. What amazes me still, to this day, is not the skill, but the coolness and confidence that little kid had. When I pushed him, he looked at me calmly, took off his coat, put down his bag, looked me in the eye, and put up his hands to fight. Wow—this kid didn't even know what my beef was, or even try to tell me to knock it off. Instead, he was "ready to rumble." After that experience, I had a bloody lip from a professional hook he gave me, and a sore crotch from a front kick to my manhood. The yard of students quickly rushed over to see us tussle, but it was a quick knockout. Thankfully, Lataya wasn't around to see our fight for her, because I would have lost it to a stronger, more skilled nine-year-old opponent. I never told my mother, because frankly, I knew I deserved what I got for picking a fight.

After I started having problems with my eyesight, I had transferred from that school, Commodore John Barry Elementary, to Overbrook Educational Center. I lost contact with just about everyone from that neighborhood school with my unplanned and sudden transfer. I often wondered what had happened to Lataya and many of my old classmates. I figured that I would probably never see her again—until one day, my mother came home and said, "Hey, I know someone who says she knows you." It turned out that Lataya was one of my mother's students. My mother must have had my picture up, and Lataya told my mom that she knew me. Toward the end of my seventh-grade year, I reconnected with her. We talked on the phone as much as our parents would allow—well, as much as her parents allowed her. As I remember it, her mother was really nice to me on the phone, especially after Lataya told her that I was an old classmate who was now blind. That was usually the ticket for me to get into the hearts of many mothers. "Andre's blind," said the young ladies, and their mothers would give me the green light to call their daughters anytime, as much as I wanted. Yippee! My mother made me use my manners to call, and that seemed to cause the hearts of mothers to bubble over with warm feelings even further. "May I please speak to...?" and mothers would relent and open the door for me to talk to their daughters. When I called Lataya, her mother responded in the friendliest of tones, traded casual hellos with me, and then passed the phone to her daughter. Lataya and I talked about our favorite songs on the radio, favorite snacks, and our favorite things to do. Lataya loved the song "Shower Me with Your Love" by Surface; Crunch and Munch popcorn; and playing basketball. And believe it or not, she said she loved me, too. We hit it off with all of our teenage pillow talk.

Then her stepfather entered the scene. He didn't care if I was blind, or that I had asked for Lataya in the nicest of ways—he was outright rude. "No!" he would say, and hang up the phone. This scared and enraged me. Why did he have to act like that? I wondered. He's trying to keep us apart.

Fortunately, that goon of a stepfather didn't stop us all the time. Lataya called me from her grandmother's house, and we talked whenever her mother allowed. We even talked about that kick-butt prodigy. "There was this guy you always would play with. I used to hate that you played with him all the time, and not me," I started to tell her. "We actually fought one time," I explained.

Then she asked, "Wait—was he a little older, with brown skin?" She gave some other descriptions I can't remember now. "Well, that was my cousin." Yikes, I felt stupid. I had approached this guy in the third grade and gotten a clobbering handed to me—all for nothing.

The summer between my seventh and eighth-grade years, we would see each other at my grandmother's house at 61st and Market. She and Dana knew each other, and would walk over to see me. In this case, it wasn't like some girl was coming to see me—just some friends. We would play Uno, talk, and laugh. Lataya loved to pick on Dana, and punch him all the time. He would react with dramatic ouches and ohs to paint the picture that he was getting severely assaulted as we sat on my grandmother's porch. But when she touched me, there was no punching going on. She liked to hold my hand. One time, I actually bought her a birthday present, and gave it to her on my grandmother's porch. Dana and my cousin Rodney were there, too. Rodney was always a jolly guy who loved to laugh and joke. He especially loved to tease me about Lataya, and would pick on me about liking her, and her liking me. "OOOOH!" he would bellow a high-pitched hoot whenever she came up in conversation. He would laugh incessantly as he played jokes on me. Well, one time, he got the laugh of a lifetime when I gave Lataya a gift of assorted seashells that I had bought while away at summer camp. I was blind, but I saw her face light up. The sound of her voice, and the appreciation that she showed was invaluable. "Stay here; I have something to give you." I left her on the porch, and went inside to get the gift.

When I came out, she said in the cheeriest voice, "Thank you." Then she grabbed my hand and didn't let go. Dana and Rodney were there, and started laughing, as goofy as teenage boys do. I was serious, and wanted them to knock it off. Then she said something to Dana in his ear. "Come here," she said to him. He started giggling even more, and the snickering and whispering amped up to another level. He rushed over to me, and in my ear, he said, "She wants to French-kiss you!"

What?! I thought, and my heart instantly began to race. I had never kissed a girl before, and now someone liked me. I wasn't ready for that. All I had done was give her a gift, and now she wanted to kiss me. I remembered what it looked like for adults to lock lips, with their heads turned to the side— and now it was my turn. After a flurry of whispers, Dana and Rodney giggled and went into the house to give us some "alone time" to get our romance "popping." She said, "Let's kiss," and dove into my face. Her lips against mine were like soft flaps of skin wiggling up and down. She moved her lips quickly, as if she were a fish at a 5 p.m. feeding. I felt like she was sucking all of the air out of my body. I was holding my breath, and thought I was going to pass out. Then Rodney came running out on the porch with the loudest, most evil "HAAAA!" I was embarrassed. He must have been watching from the inside of the house, and when he saw us kissing, he ran outside to taunt me to the 10th degree. I was so embarrassed. Leave it up to your teenage cousin and friends to be serious, and you'll be sorely disappointed.

I found kissing to be an acquired taste. That first time was weird for me, but she seemed even happier and more love-struck. I was sweating and nervous. I was just glad it was over—but she had other plans. She wanted to kiss more while we were out there. "Okay," I said, and held my breath again. She wanted to kiss again and again and again. My body was exhausted from the colony of butterflies that had been inhabiting my belly. I couldn't keep them from flying around, so needless to say, I was an emotionally drained basket case, riddled with nervousness and anxiety that afternoon. She and Dana made plans to leave, and just before she decided to go, she asked for ANOTHER kiss. We were both standing up on the porch this time, and our lips took us underwater again—but then, something terrible happened.

"Excuse me!" yelled a man's voice from the pavement in front of my grandmother's house. "Is this the Fitzgerald residence? Excuse me!" His words were more of a statement rather than a question. At the same time, behind us, I heard, "Ah, ah, what the hell!?" It was my grandmother. She had seen us kissing. At the same time, Rodney was laughing harder than you could imagine. I slipped into the house past my grandmother, waved goodbye to Lataya, and tried to gather myself. Not only had we been kissing for the first time, but my grandmother had seen it! She rushed into the house after talking to the appalled gentleman, and told me that I shouldn't allow "no gal" to get me to do anything I don't want to do! She was psychic. How did she know?

Lataya was my first girlfriend, but unfortunately, as we got older, we grew apart. She had problems at home, and our opportunities to talk were few and far between. Whenever I did get to speak to her in high school, she seemed to be changing in weird ways, and our "kiddie love" fizzled out.

In some ways, our relationship set me up for lots of disappointment for the rest of my teenage years. She had an innocent love for me that saw past my blindness. She remembered me as the little boy running around in the elementary schoolyard. She had given me the chance to be her boyfriend—but not all girls were like her. After that, my luck with the ladies was not good. Even though I was given the green light to call, many of them shied away from any teenybopper love with me. I was a "friend." I had the wonderful privilege of hearing about all the wonderful boys who were out there. I heard about the jocks, the pretty boys, and the smooth daddies. I heard about teenage rendezvous after rendezvous. I used to wonder if it was because I wasn't smooth or cute enough, but the writing was on the wall. I started to find out that some girls were scared to "go with me" or date me because I was blind.

I heard a whole host of reasons why some girls wouldn't date me. Some were explicitly stated, while others were implied.

"We can't go out because you can't drive."

"My grandmother told me we shouldn't go out because our kids could be blind."

"Would I have to take care of you?"

"You can't tell me how pretty I am."

"What would I do if people stared at us?"

"Would I have to make sure you got home safely?"

"Do you need help in the bathroom?"

These were the types of statements and questions I heard while trying to date during my teenage and young adult years. Girls and young ladies were unsure about what it would be like to date me. It was as if they thought they would miss out on so much because they had a blind boyfriend. I was an inferior product, a lemon, a gimmick. I was a semi-man, a pseudo-male, a sorta-guy. The role of men in relationships is to be the doer, the provider, the protector, and the leader; but these traits were doubted in me. I started to get the feeling that I was seen as Peter Pan, the boy who would never grow up. The zest that Lataya had shown for me was rarely seen in others. Consequently, my dating life in high school and college was devoid of any real, committed relationship. My options were limited.

I explored all kinds of ways to meet women, from online dating to tele-personals to trying to "holler" at women in the street. I explored all types of women, ranging in age, race, and ability, but it seemed like the older and more successful I became, the harder a good match was to find. By the time I was 27 years old, I had a doctorate in psychology, and that made it even more difficult. I needed to be with someone with whom I could share similar interests. Unfortunately, by that time, some were actually intimidated by my educational achievements. Those who were my equal wanted more. I was slowly limiting myself—and my dating prospects. One woman explained that she was not always nice to me because "I was giving you tough love. Since you are blind and all...I did not want to baby you. You do live with your mother, still." I was still living with my mother, but it was only because I was a full-time student with internships while in graduate school. There was no time to work. Another woman loved to mock the way I did things differently as a blind man. Still others were simply scared of the unknown.

Thankfully, I experienced a stretch in which I was getting more confident in approaching women, and striking while the iron was hot. If there was a pretty voice next to me on the bus, I struck up a conversation. If I met someone at church, I got to know them; and if I met someone in a psychology class or seminar, I talked with them about the material. Most importantly, I dared myself to be fun with women. I realized that just being a nice guy looking for an opportunity was not getting me anywhere. Instead, I had to boldly be myself.

By the time I was 28 years old, I had managed to start dating a few women, and had some good and not-so-good experiences. I basically kept knocking, and the doors opened. My confidence grew, and my understanding of what I needed and wanted in a wife also grew. I needed someone who could see me as a blind man, but also see me as a man. She would appreciate me for my zeal for life, respect me for the gifts I possessed, and be gracious when she knew I needed her help. This was tough to find.

Fortunately, I started my training in modern psychoanalysis while I was getting my doctorate. In psychoanalysis training, all of the therapists have to go through therapy; and while I was in therapy, I learned a lot about myself and what I needed in someone. I also understood that the woman I needed was going to be unlike most women. I learned what to look for—so when she finally came, I knew it was her.

After I got out of graduate school, I picked up some part-time work at Crozer Community Hospital in Chester, Pennsylvania. I worked with disadvantaged youth and their families. Many of these families also had case managers. I remember one in particular who was amazing with some of the more challenging children. One child was on her caseload as well as my own. Paul came from a family of origin in which he had been severely abused and neglected. As a result, he had been bounced from foster home to foster home. He was unable to attach to anyone—until this case manager came along. Her name was Ms. Katina Gordon. She did so well with problematic children by setting firm boundaries; but in addition, she was very generous with the attention and care she showed to every single child. She used to bring little six-year-old Paul to come see me.

One day, Paul's appointment was cancelled, and I took that time to see another parent. When the session ended, Ms. Katina rushed into my office and said, "Wait! That woman took MY time!" She began to catch my attention. Katina and I started spending lots of time on cases, talking about families. She also smelled really good. She liked to wear heels, and I got really good at knowing when she was coming down the hall toward my office. I heard click, click, click, then "Hello, Dr. Watson," in the sweetest, most smiling, sexiest voice. She always made it a point to speak to me when she saw me, in that slow, melodic voice. I was enamored.

Four important experiences with Katina told me volumes about her character, beauty, and wisdom. The first occurred when she showed up at my office with Paul, and it became apparent that she had lost her voice. She could hardly talk, and spoke in a strained whisper. When Paul asked her what had happened to her voice, she said she had been singing all weekend at her church, and had lost her voice. Church, I thought to myself. My mother would love her. And I wonder if she can sing. The mere fact that someone goes to church is not instant confirmation of a saintly disposition, but it does show they could be a person of spiritual character.

The second event took place when she came into the office with Paul after the Thanksgiving Day holiday. When Paul asked her what she had done for Thanksgiving, she bragged about cooking all weekend with her family. Wow, she enjoys spending time with her family, I thought to myself. That's a great quality to have in a partner—someone who values family.

The third experience was based upon her tenderness. One Wednesday afternoon, when she brought Paul into my office, he was being a handful. He talked back, defied redirection, and demanded all of her attention, even if that meant he would trash my office to get it. For a time, he used to try to jump on my desk, push my computer to the floor, and threaten to throw himself into a glass wall. It was not until I sternly declared to Paul that this was MY office, and he was NOT going to destroy it, that he started to settle in. My hypothesis is that he started to feel safe and protected because I took control over him, his safety, and the environment, and his parents had not done that for him. Katina also used to pick him up, but he would protest, demand a snack or McDonald's, or just refuse to cooperate. Katina was always firm with him, but loving, too.

With all of the time I had been spending with Katina, I just had to know more about her. I did a search online. It turned out that her birthday was coming. When Paul was brought to his therapy appointment on her birthday, he announced it. "Today's Ms. Katina's birthday!" I smiled and thanked her for transporting him. I shut the door to my office, and started our session. When I asked what he wanted to do that day, he said he wanted to make her a birthday card. He spent part of our session talking about how he really liked her, and wrote it all over a makeshift construction-paper birthday card he had made. When he gave it to her when our session was over, one would have thought she had won the lottery. "Oh, my goodness!" her voice squeaked with delight. "Thank you so much!" By the sound of her voice, I could tell she was hugging him as she repeated, "Thank you so much!" She and I both knew how important it was for Paul to express positive emotion, and we encouraged it. At the same time, I fell in love with her ability to appreciate a child's gift to her. This was the third of four things that stood out to me.

The fourth important feature I noticed about her became apparent when she had demanded "her time" with me when Paul didn't come one Wednesday. Instead of seeing Paul, when this happened, I would see her. I sat in my therapist's chair, she came in, and we talked. She started talking about her father, and lit up like a Christmas tree. She talked about how he was a funny man who was also a "no-nonsense" kind of guy. She smiled and became animated, and the love she had for her father was all over her. With the way she appreciates Paul and the way she appreciates her Pa, I thought, she's got to be great to her partner.

Those clicking heels and sweet hellos made quiet an impression on me, and I started to find reasons to call her to talk about cases. Soon, she started finding reasons to come into my office. Before we knew it, our schedules were in sync, and we were seeing a lot of each other.

Before we took an interest in one other, I had been pursued by another woman in a different department. It had been a nightmare, and involved being repeatedly stood up by the woman, who begged me to come see her and to be patient with her. After realizing she was a total head case, I moved on to look for someone sane. In consequence, I became totally against dating anyone on the job—but there was something so compelling and captivating about Katina.

Valentine's Day arrived not too long after her birthday, and I just had to send her something. My mother had once told me that my father used to send her flowers when they were together, and that always stuck with me, both as a child and as an adult. I often sent flowers to my mother and to the women I was dating, and this Valentine's Day was no exception. I decided to send her roses, and said in the card, "Someone adores you, and thinks you are oh-so-sweet." The next day, she smiled at me even harder than she usually did, and stood closer to me when we spoke in my office. I had the feeling that she might have known, but I was too trauma- tized from the girl who had come before her, and was quite okay with keeping my secret to myself.

A couple of days passed before my cellphone rang while I was at work. It was the florist, and they said, "Dr. Watson, we are calling you because you sent flowers to Ms. Katina Gordon on February 14th. She is calling to find out who sent the flowers, Sir."

I replied, "No, do not tell her," and hung up. They kept calling me back that day, and told me that she kept calling them. When they called a fourth time on my way home, I hesitantly told them to give her my number. She called, and said with a smile and happy curiosity, "Yes...who is this?" I replied in my deepest, most businesslike voice, "This is Dr. Watson. May I help you?" She burst out laughing, and the rest is history.

We started dating, became engaged 20 months later, and were married nine months after that. We had a wonderful courtship. It was so easy to go out with her and enjoy dinner, the movies, plays, the beach, and comedy shows. I often made her laugh, and I was shocked at how funny she thought I was. She turned out to be the woman I thought she was: incredibly appreciative, undeniably trustworthy, and unbelievably caring. Our dates weren't filled with critical talk or negative comments, and they were always uplifting, lighthearted, and full of substance. We shared a passion for treating children and families, and realized that we had a lot in common. And I was right—she was good with Paul, great to her father, and absolutely gorgeous with me. She seemed to respect me and value my professional and personal opinions. What was so wonderful about loving her was that I could see that she loved me, too.

My blindness was not off-putting or depressing to her. She seemed very comfortable when talking about my blindness, and discussing all that I had accomplished. She bragged to her family and friends about me. Many asked about what we did, and what it was like dating me. She insisted that it was wonderful. She told them that I made all of the plans for our dates, and even took her around Philadelphia, with which she was unfamiliar. She boasted about her newfound opportunities to take trains, trolleys, and taxis with me.

Katina was from Chester, Pennsylvania—a small town that allowed her to drive everywhere. There had been no big-city living going on in Chester, where people talk about going to Philadelphia as if it were a field trip to a faraway city—even though Chester is 15 minutes away on the highway. Katina was happy that someone else was doing the driving.

On one of our first dates, she told me, "I want to go to places the way you go. Let's take the bus." I was floored. For years, I had been denied the opportunity to take prospective girlfriends out because they were just too cute to take public transportation. Here was a woman who trusted me to take her on public transportation, into a city she hardly knew.

We have since traveled to the Jersey Coast, the Caribbean, Spain, Puerto Rico, Italy, and many other places because she has let me take us places. Once, she told a friend of hers about me competing in the 2008 Paralympics in China. This friend kept asking, "Who's going to take care of him?" and "Why aren't you going with him?"

She told them, "He gets around better than me. I need his help."

I often wonder how Katina can see me as a capable person in spite of my disability. It's not uncommon for me to struggle to prove myself to others, in many arenas; and even though I've become highly successful, there are still doubters. Katina has always seemed to believe in me, my mind, and my ability to be a man—even though I have a "disability." I believe that this is strongly connected to her relationship with her mother and father.

Katina's father, Mr. Gordon, was one of 13 children raised on a farm in Opelousas, Louisiana. He tells scores of stories about how hard he worked on his family's farm. He boasts of carrying trees on his back for $5 a week, picking cotton in the snow, and being able to hunt anything on four legs. I once overheard him talking to a pal of his. The friend said, "We had it tough when I was a kid. I remember getting shoes once a year. Our shoes had holes in them."

Mr. Gordon simply responded, "What...? Who had shoes?" He lived a physically demanding childhood and young adulthood. As a result, he was an incredibly muscular man with a rock-hard body, an alpha male with a chip on his shoulder if anyone doubted his strength or determination. Katina saw him work long, hard days. She said she knows a man works hard when he comes home and smells like it. She has tales of him being able to fix anything, and lift anything; and, in her mind, he could and can still do anything. Her daddy is everything to her.

With all of that said, Katina also saw his challenges, struggles, and vulnerabilities. One in particular was his inability to be well organized as he went to school up to the sixth grade. Since he was from a family in which boys worked on the farm and girls went to school, he'd hardly had the opportunity of a formal education. As a result, he became a very sharp, observant man, always three steps ahead of everyone else. He can anticipate other people's decisions and the steps they will choose to take, either on the job or in his personal life. He figures out how to survive in spite of his struggle. Katina often says that while she was growing up, he would gaze at her homework, acting as if he was a professor. He would say things like, "That's good," or "No, that's not right," or "Fix that, you know that ain't right." She said that he was always correct.

Even now, she doesn't know how he did it; and for the longest time, she never knew he was not as organized as her. After she got older, she began helping him with the organization of important documents. These documents sit in a tin box in his home, and when he needs to revisit some financial or medical information, he pulls it out so she can read the papers to him over and over again. She says lovingly, "Oh no, here's that box again." She would read him the information and reorganize the papers. When he would bring her the box the next time, the papers would be disorganized. He had been shuffling them around, trying to make sense of them.

I have a box, too. When we first got married, I started pulling that box out. "Sweetheart, I need to find our tax returns," I'd say, or, "Katina, can you help me find those insurance papers?" or, "Did you say the copy of the instructions was in this pile?" She can't help but laugh.

Our wedding song was "Made to Love You" by Gerald Levert. And in so many ways, we were made to love each other. She was raised by a strong, emotionally intelligent, relentless, hardworking mother and father, and she married a similar man. Her childhood with a great father with flaws made her a better woman and wife. So many of my clients who have not grown up with fathers look for men who are perfect, and have little tolerance for flaws or shortcomings. They run at any potential issue. I believe this comes from not having a realistic view of a man, and not knowing what to expect.

Katina knows how to love a man with a soothing gentleness that is accepting and encouraging. She's the wife I want to work hard and sacrifice myself for. She's a life partner who's in it to the end. She does not bail out when times get tough. My wife is a real woman.

So many people have problems finding love. Many times, it's because they don't even know what they are looking for in a mate. They say, "tall, dark, and handsome," or "sweet and petite." Others use buzzwords like "kind, friendly, and outgoing," but few really know what to look for.

It is important to be ready to love someone—and to be loved. I had a rough road, and grew to appreciate someone who appreciated me. I had been denied for all sorts of stupid reasons, and I knew that the woman who picked me was going to be the smart one. I was going to make sure she would never regret the decision to be with me. I was going to be on my A-Game, follow through with reliability, treat her like a queen, and be her best friend. I knew that choosing someone who loved and had a good relationship with her parents was going to boost my chances of being happy. Most people have parents with many flaws, and often, we are stuck with the baggage of the ways we were disappointed by them. Until we can heal from these disappointments, it's going to be really hard to be with someone. I noticed that Katina loved her father to pieces. He was her knight in shining armor; and when I saw her potential to love, I knew I wanted to feel that love from her.

So many people are hooked on their physical sight, and allow outer appearances to throw them a curveball. For me, loving in the dark has been a freeing experience. It has been so much easier to let go of worry about the approval of others. It occurred to me while dating: Why do I even ask what a woman looks like from a friend? I cannot see her anyway, and until I get to see her for myself, I won't know if she will be for me. Often, we hope that our friends will approve, or that our parents will okay the relationship; and as a result, we end up trying too hard to make others happy.

When do we close our eyes in life—not only in romantic relationships, but in relationships in general—how many times do we find that we have prejudged others based upon superficialities and popular opinion? I knew who I was when I met my wife. I didn't need physical sight to know she was adorable, beautiful, and oh, so sweet.

ABOUT DR. ANDRE WATSON

Dr. Andre Watson received his undergraduate degree at the University of Pittsburgh, where he majored in psychology and minored in Spanish and Africana studies. He then went on to earn his master's and doctoral degrees in clinical psychology from Widener University in Chester, Pennsylvania. He is a senior candidate at the Philadelphia School of Psychoanalysis and is working towards being a certified psychoanalyst.

Dr. Watson runs his own private practice where he specializes in strengthening and mending relationships within families, as well as in treating children and adolescents to cope with life's hardships and misfortunes. Dr. Watson is also a motivational speaker, author, and leader in the blindness community. He facilitates an adjustment to blindness group for blind adolescents, and does self-defense presentations for various organizations designed to serve the blind community. Dr. Watson teaches psychology courses to adult learners at the University of Phoenix's Philadelphia, Ground Campus.

Dr. Watson's athletic achievements are numerous over the past 25 years. To just name a few achievements, He was Third Team All Public and Sportsman of the year in high school wrestling. Additionally, he has won three national championships with the Pennsylvania Tornado Goalball team and was named to the United States national goalball team in 2002. He held a spot on the Paralympic judo team from 2005 to 2008, and competed in the 2008 Paralympics in Beijing, China, representing the United States. He was the Pennsylvania Master's Judo champion in 2009 among sighted fighters and U.S. Master's Bronze Medalist in 2009 among sighted fighters. He is one of the founders and the first president of the Audio Dart Club of Delaware Valley. Lastly, Dr. Watson is currently learning Brazilian Jujitsu to add to his repertoire of martial arts.

Dr. Watson is married to his lovely wife Katina and is a proud father of his five-year-old daughter, Kenya. In his free time, he enjoys playing his guitar, working out in his home gym, playing hide-and-seek with Kenya, spending time with his family, and traveling with Katina.

43235304R00096

Made in the USA
Middletown, DE
04 May 2017